THE MASON WOODS

By

PHILLIP V. MAZZILLI

United States Library of Congress COPYRIGHT Pending 2/2010

ISBN: 978-0-615-35783-6

This book is dedicated to the memory of my lovely wife of 54 years, Ursela - 7.28.1926 – 9.11.2009. who missed seeing 'The Mason Woods' completed by less then three months.

She was my close and constant companion and is missed dearly.

Table of Contents

Prologue

This book captures a brief time in our history that in my mind may never occur again. It is possible that other children during this time period experienced similar lives of excitement and innocence. And to those who have lived through similar experiences, this book will bring back many memories. This book is a work in creative non-fiction.

Mason Woods is about the bond of friendship that developed between three young boys Boo, Johnny and Phil at a time in America when family and dependency on friendship was very important. It was a time when the advanced technologies were the radio, the automobile and the movies. The aspirations of every parent were basically the same as those today and that is to see their children succeed by entering establishments of higher learning and finding their niche in society. Education was of prime importance to all growing up during this time.

Mason Woods tells of the hardships encountered by the people who chose to immigrate to The United States from the poverty stricken areas of Europe. It is based on fact as told to the author by the people who lived through and experienced the hardships of coming to a new land, their chosen land, The United States of America.

Although it is about two families, these same experiences and hardships were prevalent among all immigrants of that time.

Isabella and Vito came to the U.S.A. from small towns in Southern Italy. Poverty in Southern Italy was extensive after WWI. Those who did not own a plot of land worked for farmers who had olive trees, almond trees or wheat fields. Commerce at that time was at a virtual stand still.

WWI had drained Italy of its young men. Vito turned eighteen towards the end of the war and was subject to the Draft. He was drafted into the Italian Cavalry in September of 1918. WWI ended in November of that same year.

Isabella's view of WWI was seen through the eyes of a child being 10 years old when the war ended. The small community she lived in was on a mountain side and isolated from the ravages of war. Her knowledge of the war was seeing young men being drafted to fight and to a lesser extent the reduction in food supplies available to the citizens. Since her Mother was ill and being the oldest, Isabella had to drop out of school after the fourth grade to help raise her brothers and sisters. Isabella never forgave her Mother for causing her to cut her education short to raise the family.

I am eternally indebted to both to have chosen to

immigrate to this land of freedom and unlimited opportunity. And for choosing to reside near the Mason Woods.

The Mason Woods

Chapter 1

The Setting

The tractor putt-putted towards the huge oak tree. Smoke bellowing from its exhaust pipe that stood three feet above the drivers cab. It laid its blade on the side of the trunk and pushed forward. Crows, robins, cardinals and other small birds flew in every direction away from the tree. Fluttering. Whistling. Screeching. The engine roared loudly. Its tracks digging ever deeper into the soft earth until the tree gave way. The tractor engine stalled but it had done its work.

The old oak tree came crashing down towards the forest floor. Branches as big as tree trunks snapped. The splintering wood sounded like gunshots. The echoes bounced through the forest and the deep hollow. The ancient tree settled on the bed of the forest. It lay still. The forest was unusually quiet as if paying respect to the ancient oak with it's silence. The natural spring that gurgled from beneath its massive trunk since time immemorial, forever sealed. The youthful memories of past generations were sealed with it. Never more to provide that welcomed cool satisfying sip for children and hunters, as it had for an untold number of years.

Maybe even centuries.

The year is 1953. Progress has started to take its toll on nature. The tractor started up and putt putted loudly as it backed away from the felled tree. Black smoke engulfed the driver. The tractor turned and went on towards other trees. A new community will soon be covering the area at the beginning of the Mason Woods. Eventually, the Woods will be no more.

My name is Phillip. Everyone calls me Phil except Mom. Mothers are funny that way. I am a ten-year-old boy growing up in the early 1940s. I consider myself a typical inquisitive friendly boy with brownish hair and a very slim build. I grew up during a time when everything seems to be right with the known world. The known world to me during these early years extended to the far edges of the small city that I lived in and the Mason Woods that lay on the edge of the city. Beyond was the unknown. There is no television. I am free to experience all the things that are important to young boys. Playing tag, hide and seek, baseball and football. Most importantly learning to get along with the neighborhood children. Sometimes this is a problem. When you have an argument, it is hard to be friends with that person. He is your enemy for life. Well, at least until school starts in the fall or a new game of tag, whichever comes first?

Our small city has 8,124 residents. Though there are many ethnic groups the majority are Italian immigrants or first generation of Italian immigrants. Our neighborhood consists of sixteen Italian, two

Yugoslavian and one Hungarian family. They all exchanged greetings when passing on the street. The houses on the street were all free standing and basically constructed of wood siding with "V-shaped" roofs and shingles made from tar. None was any more expensive then the next one. Basically, we were all poor. We lived in peace and harmony.

Two rivers merge at the East edge of downtown. The river flowing towards the South is a place where the locals fish. The catch is usually carp or catfish. The concrete dam that stands eight feet tall and is two hundred feet wide allows the water to accumulate behind it. The water cascades slowly over the dam creating a beautiful glassy waterfall. The water comes from a man made lake 15 miles North of the waterfalls. The water is usually crystal clear. It does cloud up with silt after a hard rain. In winter some fool hardy young people ice skate on the river near the falls. The flowing water makes for thin ice. There have been several drownings over the years.

In the summer of 1941 a few people use the clean river as a swimming hole. On one hot Sunday afternoon, Mom, Dad, my younger Brother Johnny and I went to the river to swim. Dad had this bright red woolen one-piece bathing suit. It was a combined t-shirt and shorts kind of thing that covered all but the arms and legs with large round holes on each side of the t-shirt. Johnny and I wore our regular everyday shorts and Mom sat on a nearby tree stump and watched.

Dad was first in the water. Johnny and I hesitated.

"C'mon boys! Jump in the water!" Dad said as he made swimming motions and noise to show how much he was enjoying himself.

"This water is nice and cool! C'mon!"

Mom coaxed us "Go in the water! You don't have to worry! Your Father is a good swimmer! Look! See how he swims!"

"Wait! I'll come and help you!"

Dad came to the edge and took each of our hands and helped us into the water.

"Now you have your feet wet, come out a little bit farther, but not too far!"

Johnny and I eased into the river water up to our belly buttons and decided not to go any farther.

"Do you want to learn how to swim? I'll teach you!"

Dad took each of us and held us in the water and instructed us on how to move our arms and legs.

After a little bit of that we began to just stand there waist deep in the water and splash each others for about any hour while Dad swam.

"OK! I think that its time for us to go kids!" Mom said.

Obediently we got out of the water with Dad following.

Mom then began to dry us off and get us dressed.

There were many other parents and children in the river. It was fun. Dad seemed to enjoy it more than Johnny and me. We returned home. We enjoyed riding in the 1932 Model A Ford that he was very proud of. With the windows rolled down catching the breeze was very refreshing.

The second river is polluted from the dumping of materials into it by the regional steel mills. The mills used the river water to cool the red-hot steel that was being manufactured into various useable forms. The cooling process took tons of water. This water was returned to the river with iron chips and dust that was released from the steel. These particles settled all along the river and turned the color of the river to a rusty red. It's such a waste to let the clean water go into and mix with the water that is polluted. The rivers flow southward to join a third river many miles away.

There is a park on the West Side of downtown with an Olympic sized pool. From home the city pool is a four-mile ride on my bike. The cost to enter the pool is a nickel. Of course the wages at this time average about ten dollars for forty hours of work. If you could find the work! That's twenty-five cents for one hour of labor. The pool is filled with clean chlorinated water that is changed every Friday morning. Negroes are not allowed in the pool for six days during the week. On Thursdays, they have the pool to themselves for free. We tried to get in to swim for free but Old Bill Llewellyn, the Parks and Recreation Director for the city would not let us in. He told us to come back tomorrow when the water was changed. There are only five Negro families in the city at this time. I go to school with two of their children, James and Henrietta.

The downtown is made up of three major streets. Main Street is the larger in terms of the number of storefronts. Most of the storefronts are well maintained. The owners do take pride in their community. There is a mixture of red brick and concrete buildings. The red brick buildings are the older buildings.

Main Street has two movie theaters. The McKinley Theater and the Robbins Theater. Both are relatively new. The two main features of the downtown are located on Main Street.

The first main feature is a bank building that is seven stories high. It has the only elevator in town. For my friends who heard of the New Empire State Building in New York City, this was the second tallest building anywhere.

The second main feature is the pride of the city a large white marble monument to President William McKinley. Inside is a huge public library and meeting rooms. I spend a lot of time in the library. There is a lot of interesting stuff there. I hope that someday I will be able to write something that will be on file in the library. The second floor of the library has old newspaper files and an area with stereoscopes for viewing pictures in three dimension. Looking at the stereo photographs was fun. The open rotunda in the center of the library facility has a large statue of the President. Standing. Observing the vista beyond the monument, made up of a large grassy area and a monster white marble walkway leading to the front steps. Huge colonnades support the marble ring surrounding the open top of the rotunda. The statue is surrounded with plants and flowers.

It is said that during his childhood President McKinley lived on Main St. where the Monument stands. Others say that he lived where the McKinley Bank stands, within a row of storefronts along Main St.

There are three banks in the downtown. For the size of the population, the downtown is fairly large. W. State Street is where the local newspaper The Daily Times and the Municipal building are located. W. State Street crosses Main Street and then curves to the left at a ninety-degree angle paralleling Main Street then becomes E. State Street and ends at Robbins Avenue. Before reaching the Park Ave. intersection on the left side is the new Greyhound Bus Terminal that was recently completed. Between the Bus Station and Park Ave. is the Warner Theater, the older of the three theaters in town.

Beyond Park Ave, on the right side is Central Park. The trees in the park are oak, elm and maple. In the center of the park, surrounded by a sidewalk with dark green painted slat benches, is a huge fountain. On top of the fountain, is a copper replica of the Statue of Liberty. From the extended arm holding the torch large volumes of water shoot into the air. The water washes over the statue into a large round copper holding dish that surrounds the center stem of the fountain. Then down into a larger copper dish and finally into the pool. The pool is one hundred feet in diameter, three feet deep at its center, and one and one half feet at its edge. The copper center stem, the dishes and statue atop the fountain have a beautiful grayish green color from years of oxidizing. The sound of the water cascading into the pool breaks the silence of the park.

The air, cooled by the falling water creates a breeze that swirls into the area under the trees. On a hot day, this is the coolest place in town. In the summer there is always someone wading in the shallows of the pool, pants legs folded up above the knees or skirt wrapped around the thighs held tight with one hand. Of course there was always the occasional hero who would try unsuccessfully to climb the fountain.

The common transportation of the time is walking. Walking is in style. People are always walking through Central Park or sitting on the benches, enjoying the cool air. You could always find someone sitting and quietly taking in the peaceful atmosphere of the park. At dusk, the park is enveloped in a cozy warm light. The fountain is lit up making the water shimmer as it falls to the pool below. The walkways with beautiful lantern type lighting, add to the inviting glow of the fountain. The only sound is that of the cascading water.

In the fall the pump that feeds the water to the fountain is turned off. Colored leaves fall from the Maple trees into the pool and cover the water. The leaves form a colorful carpet of crimsons and yellows. The Statue of Liberty atop the fountain is still.

In the winter the fountain and the pool are drained. The winter freeze could crack the fountain and the pool if the water is allowed to remain in them. The fountain is turned back on in mid June.

The storefronts on E. State Street are few and not maintained as well as the Main Street storefronts. This is sort of the back end of the city and does not get the higher traffic that the stores on Main Street get. Park Ave. is where the fire station, the police station and the post office are located. The Post Office is always busy.

Residential areas spread out from the downtown in all directions. The East Side is where the most people live. That's where I live. All the main roads leading from downtown and the downtown streets are paved with firebrick, the road construction material of the time.

To the East and to the West of our city are two larger cities. The trolley, sometimes called the streetcar, on it's way to either, passes through our city. It makes stops to pickup passengers at pickup points on its journey. The streetcar is slowly being phased out in favor of the new mode of mass transportation, the Greyhound Bus. The rails buried in the streets and the overhead wires that provide the trolley with power, are in the process of being removed. Automobiles are not the chief mode of transportation at this time.

The Mason Woods

Chapter 2

Immigration of Vito

Vito was the oldest of five children. He was in the service for several weeks, when he received word that his Father was on his deathbed. Hardly having become accustomed to the ways of the military he was given leave to go to his family in Corato, Italy. Corato is on the Adriatic side of Italy. It is inland from the seashore.

While on leave, his Father passed away and the war ended on November 11, 1918. Having been in the Cavalry for such a short time and thinking he was no longer needed he did not go back. After several months, in August of 1919, he got word that he was AWOL (Absent With Out Leave) and that the military was looking for him. He had made an error in thinking he was automatically discharged when the war ended. It was at this moment Vito decided to leave his mother his brother and two sisters. Time to leave his country and go to his sister in the United States. It was very distressing for his mother who had just lost her husband and was now losing her oldest son.

Vito's younger brother Michele is left with the task of looking after and providing for the family. There would be hard times ahead, but Vito made a promise to them that he would send money from the United States to help them. He said his goodbyes to his family and told them that he would not contact them until he arrived in The United States. His plan was to go to Genoa and from there he would take a ship to the United States. Stressed by the thought of leaving his family and country behind, with the small bag that his Mother had packed, Vito began his journey by going westward to Rome.

During his first week on the road he is tempted to return to Corato and await the punishment of the military. He rationalized that this would also take him away from his family. He persevered and continued with his plan. It took him two months, stopping in small villages along the way and working a day or two for a place to sleep and something to eat. Mostly he sleeps in barns and was given whatever food the farmer's wife was feeding the family. He was thankful for any help that he was given. During the long days he worries about his family and about this journey that he has undertaken. He is driven by the need to leave the country or suffer the consequences of his error in judgment.

In November of 1919, Vito arrived in Rome. The weather was becoming cooler. Fall was in the air. He spent three weeks in Rome, going to the Vatican and the Coliseum among other attractions of Ancient Rome. He was amazed at the size of St Peters Basilica. He was able to climb the stairs to the cupola and view Rome from above. The wind was brisk. He stayed until the cold began biting at his nose. As he moved through the Basilica his eyes widened at the site of the Pieta. The Sistine Chapel left him speechless. How could Michelangelo lying on his back make such beautiful paintings? It brought a tear to his eyes. How could one man make so much beauty? He was truly a gifted man.

Rome is a large city and it is easy to get lost in the crowd. There are people continually moving around everywhere. He knows that it would be difficult to be identified and returned to the military while in Rome. But he continues to keep a low profile. He avoids the Carabinieri whenever he spots them. The possibility of being caught and turned over to the military is always on his mind. He is, so to speak, running and hiding. Vito worked for food and a few Lire, the Italian currency. He confided in the people he did work for. They sympathized with him and gave him a little extra to help him on his journey.

Vito left Rome on a sunny morning in early December. There was a definite chill in the air. The warmth of the sun felt good on his back as he headed due west to the Tyrrhenian Sea. His mind was full of thoughts of what he had seen in Rome and how friendly the Romans were to him. He would never forget this brief but pleasant experience.

Reaching the Sea he turned north. Following the roads along the coast, he began his trek towards Pisa. This leg of his trip was the most difficult as there was not much movement of traffic going north. Most of his travel was on foot. January was a cold month. Fortunately he met people along the way that fed him, give him work and invited him to sleep in their house so that he could be out of the cold. At each stop he had to tell them why such a young man was on the road in such cold weather. As he proceeded, his thoughts became more focused on going to the United States and a new life. He celebrated his twentieth birthday several days outside of Pisa. In mid February of 1920, two and one half months after leaving Rome he arrived in Pisa.

In Pisa he was moved at the site of the Leaning Tower. Most Italians of that time had only heard of the Leaning Tower and few had seen it. Italy was basically a very poor nation and WWI did not help to improve the Italian situation.

After making stops along the way in more Italian cities as La Spetzia, doing odd jobs to provide food for himself, he arrived in Genoa the thriving Italian Seaport in late March of 1920. Here he would work and save money for passage to the United States. He knew that he had to be very careful in Genoa since this would be the last place where he could still be apprehended and shipped to the stockade. His family was always on his mind. He wondered how they were handling their situation back home without him. He knew that he must be brave for himself and for them. He picked up odd jobs and began putting away his Lire.

Six weeks later, in mid May, he took the money he had earned and made his way down to the docks.

Vito made many inquiries about vessels going to The

United States. A person that he befriended while working at the dock loading cargo onto the ships confronted him at the dock.

"Vito! I need to tell you something. Last night I was with an older friend named Cosmo who lives here in Genoa. Cosmo has been working at the docks for many years. I told him about you and your wanting to go to America."

"And what did he have to say, Filippo?"

"He said that during the war when he was working on the docks, they used to pick up men who did not want to serve in the Army, when they went to buy their boarding ticket for the boat. The ticket agent would call the Carabinieri and they would take the persons away to jail! In your case, you would most likely be identified as being AWOL, arrested by the Carabinieri and sent back to the Cavalry to spend time in the stockade. "

"What should I do?"

"Cosmo said that what you should do to be safe is go to Marseilles. There the Italian government cannot stop you. It is the safest thing that you can do, Vito!"

"Many thanks Filippo and thank Cosmo for me to. I will leave Genoa today."

Disappointed and tired, his dream of leaving from Genoa was shattered. He was faced with having to continue his journey before he could board a ship to The United States. An exhausted Vito pulled himself together and slowly made his way Westward to Marseilles, France.

After one year of walking and hitching farmers cart

rides from Southern Italy into France, in mid August of 1920 he arrived in Marseilles, France. He was a worn man. The trip had taken its toll spiritually. He would not be able to stand another set back. Marseilles is in Southern France on the Mediterranean Sea.

Vito had money that he had saved in Genoa. It was not enough to pay for his fare. Vito made friends and did odd jobs to supplement his cash shortage. After a month went by, while hauling goods on to a ship he met the Captain of the ship SS Roussillon. The ship was bound for the Port of New York. The Captain was Italian and from Corato, Italy Vito's' hometown.

"Captain! May I speak with you! I understand that you are also from Corato!"

"Yes! Is that were you are from?"

"Yes Captain!"

"What is a young man like you doing in Marseilles? So far away from your family!"

He told the Captain his problem, including being AWOL from the Italian Cavalry and his desire to go to America.

"I understand. Do you have the fare to go aboard my ship?"

"How much will I need? Asked Vito.

"For third class fare it is 2355 Francs!"

"I have more then that already! I have almost 4000 Francs!" said Vito.

The Captain placed him on the manifest of passengers bound for the United States. Vito's mind was set at ease. He anxiously awaited the day he would board the ship and leave behind his fears of being incarcerated.

The S.S. Roussillon was built by A. G. Weser Shipbuilders in 1906 for the North German company, Lloyd. Under the German flag, it was named Goeben. Its start up service was sailing from Bremerhaven, Germany to the Far East. It was in storage during WWI and was given as war reparations to the French in late 1919. The French renamed it Roussillon. It began its France-New York service in September of 1920. It sailed for ten years and was placed in storage in 1930. It was scrapped in 1931.

On the 28th of September 1920 the SS Roussillon set sail on its maiden voyage as a ship under the flag of France, leaving Marseilles for its first of many trips to New York. Vito was finally on his way to his destination The United States of America. He left his homeland and family and was now focused on what lay ahead in his life. A new beginning. He felt proud to have accomplished this on his own at the young age of 20. He was both sad and happy. Sad to be saying goodbye to his homeland and family and happy that he would not be going to the stockade. He was relieved.

The voyage began calmly. The passengers were all focused on their destination, the Port of New York that was two weeks away. You could see sadness and tears on the faces of the passengers as their thoughts focused on their homeland and what they were leaving behind. There were not many words spoken as they passed through the Straits of Gibraltar and into the Atlantic Ocean.

Leaving the calm of the Mediterranean, the rough seas of the Atlantic began to toss the vessel about. The ship was then filled with seasick people who were mostly farmers and not accustomed to the motions of a ship at sea. Vito knew that as long as he focused on the horizon, he would not become seasick. So he did not get seasick. The ships engine room crew reported to the Captain that the vessels engines were not sounding the way they should. The Captain took the information under advisement and pressed on.

Towards the end of the second day the Captain realized that there were major repairs required to the vessel. The Ships Engineer made an assessment of the parts needed to make the repair and gave the list to the Captain. The Captain had the information radioed to the mainland so the parts would be on their way to the SS Roussillon before they landed in the Canary Islands.

Partially crippled, he turned the ship towards the closest land the Canary Islands. The Canary Islands are located South-West of Spain and North-West of Africa, directly due West of the coast of Morocco. The geographical location of the Canary Islands has made it an important station for navigating between Europe, Asia and America.

The SS Roussillon docked at the Port of Santa Cruz de Tenerife on October 3rd. There the ship stayed in Port for eleven days awaiting parts needed to make the repair to arrive from the mainland. Since the documents necessary for disembarking were not available for the passengers, they had to remain on board until the ship sailed. This did not sit well with most of the passengers. The ship was crowded and they felt incarcerated. The passengers walked the decks of the small ship for exercise. The captain assured them that he was doing everything possible to get under way. The ship was serviced continuously providing necessary food and drink as the passengers waited.

There was not much to do on board. The passengers spent most of their time talking with fellow passengers. Learning where they came from and where their final destination was in The United States. Early on, Vito met a family of four who befriended him. One was a young lady about Vito's age who was very good looking. Vito was enamored. They got along well. They spent much time together during these days of waiting for the ship to get underway. They became more than friends in the short time that they spent together.

Repairs made and the Roussillon again seaworthy, the Captain set sail for New York on the 13th of October 1920 amidst the shouts and screams of joy from the passengers. The ships deep horn sounded continuously as they moved from the Port into the Atlantic Ocean. The black smoke billowing from the smoke stack as they moved full speed ahead. Things returned to normal or as normal as it could be for first time voyagers. Except for the seasickness on board, the rest of the trip was uneventful.

Vito spent most of his time with the young lady and

her family. The days spent on board were long. The view was constant. On October 23rd Vito and the young lady had their first sight of the Statue of Liberty together off the port bow of the S.S.Roussillon. Vito knew they had finally arrived in New York. The United States of America. The passengers were yelling and screaming. The men had tears in their eyes. The women wept freely.

Vito disembarked with the family that had befriended him when they arrived at Ellis Island. After all passengers had disembarked it was necessary for all to be evaluated physically for any diseases or sickness. Vito remained close to the family he had come to know. When the physical examinations were completed, it was found that the young ladies mother had tuberculosis and could not be admitted into the United States. The Father not knowing what to do decided that the family had to stay together so they would return to Marseilles on the SS Roussillon. Vito and the young lady said their goodbyes. Vito was heart broken as he left Ellis Island. Alone. His thoughts returning to his family in Corato and hoping that they were all well.

In order to enter the U.S.A. you must have a sponsor in the U.S.A. Vito's sponsor was his Aunt and her husband Michele Ruffini of Arnold, Pennsylvania a suburb of Pittsburgh. Vito found his way to Grand Central Station from Ellis Island by getting directions as he walked. It took him several hours to get there. Once in the Station, he was confronted with the problem of exchanging his Francs into Dollars. And again, by finding people who spoke

Italian he was able to exchange his money and get help to purchase a train ticket to Arnold, Pennsylvania.

His Aunt and Uncle were overjoyed to see him.

"Vito! Vito! It's so good to see you and hear your voice!" as his Aunt Francis hugged and kissed him.

"We were so worried that something happened to you. We thought that we would never see you again."

"Well Zia. It's a long story!"

He told them the entire story of his dilemma with the military, his trek across Italy and France and the boat ride. They were amazed at what he had gone through on his voyage to the United States. Vito told them about Rome and the beautifully painted ceiling in the Sistine Chapel, the massive size of St. Peters Basilica. Neither of his relatives had seen either place. They had never been to Rome. Vito talked about the Leaning Tower of Pisa and how he felt climbing to the top and looking over the leaning side, feeling as though the entire building would topple over any minute.

Vito was the center of attention as his Aunt and Uncle sat and listened to every word he spoke. He told them about meeting this beautiful girl on board ship and the disaster of the family having to return to Italy.

"Vito! We have been getting many letters from your Mama. She and your sisters and brother are very worried about you! You have to write to them right away so that they know that you are safe."

"I will write to them tomorrow morning after I get some rest."

They rejoiced until the wee hours of the morning.

The next day Vito with pen in hand sat down and wrote a five page letter to his Mother and family, explaining what had happened and apologizing for not being able to write sooner to give them information. He told his mother that he had seen the beauty of Italy during his travel to come to the United States. He promised his mother that he would write again when he got to Cleveland where his Sister and her husband lived.

Vito remained in Arnold for two weeks relaxing and getting the anxiety of his Voyage out of his system. He had not realized how much stress he had been under for the many months he was on the go continuously pursuing his goal of coming to the United States. During his stay his Uncle took him on a walking tour of downtown Pittsburgh. Dad was not impressed by the tons of smoke in the air from the surrounding factories. He said that all the buildings looked as if covered in soot. And they were. His Uncle said that it is just something that you learn to live with.

Vito then left for Cleveland, Ohio to be with his sister and her husband, Joe Mandato. There were tears of joy as the siblings embraced. Vito once more repeated the specifics of his voyage to his Sister and Brother-in-law. They were in awe. They had also received letters from Corato wondering if they had heard anything. Vito told them that he wrote to his mother immediately from Arnold. After several days living with his Sister she helped him look for work and also to find an apartment close to where she lived. Here Vito was able to settle in on the East side of Cleveland near his Sister.

After one week, Vito found a job that was to his liking. Vito took a job on a large vegetable farm outside of town that employed twenty workers. His mode of transportation was the trolley or streetcar as they were called. Each day he got aboard the streetcar at four in the morning. It took one hour on the streetcar to go to the farm. His job as well as the job of the other workers was to take care of the vegetable plants. It was all manual labor that Vito enjoyed doing. His young life in Corato evolved around farming. Working with plants was a joy for him. His belief was that the Earth was the most important thing in life. It originated life by allowing seeds to grow. It gave us all the nutrients to sustain life. And in the end all goes back to the ground. He found joy in getting his hands into the soil and hoeing the ground around the individual plants and applying fertilizer to keep them growing. Vito along with the other workers harvested and boxed the various vegetables to prepare them to be taken to market.

The owner Mr. Anthony Roberto who was Italian saw that Vito was very diligent and expressed himself very well. Mr. Roberto also noticed that Vito came in on the streetcar every morning from Cleveland and also caught the streetcar every night at seven to return home.

After his second month on the job Mr. Roberto

approached Vito.

"Vito! I have been watching your work here and I see that you like your work very much. You treat each plant like it is one of your children and I like that. You are the best worker that I have. My other workers are good. They know what they are doing but you are my best worker."

"Thank you Mr. Roberto. Thank you very much!"

"My reason for talking to you like this is I need someone to oversee the other workers. I can no longer do it by myself. My health is not to good. It would please me very much if you would oversee the other workers. There will be more money for you. Do you want the job?"

"Yes! I would like to help you. And you know that I will not let you down!"

That afternoon Mr. Roberto gathered his workers and with Vito by his side announced that Vito would be the boss and that anything that he told them would be exactly is if it came from him.

"Is there anything that you would like to say Vito?"

"Yes! Thank You Mr. Roberto for the chance to help you. And men, I have watched each one of you do your jobs and I know that Mr. Roberto has a fine crew working for him and I would like for each of you to do the same for me. As long as you do your job you will have no trouble with me."

"Now lets go back to work."

Most of the workers were immigrants from Italy. In

the next several weeks Vito became very friendly with the owners children who were students at the local high school. Mr. Roberto seeing that his family was happy with his selection of a leader for his farm asked Vito if he would take a room in his large house so he did not have to go back and forth to Cleveland. Vito jumped at the offer. This was turning out to be a great opportunity for him.

While living on the farm, the owner's children began to teach Vito English. They found him to be a rapid learner. Within six months he was able to read and converse in English. He became one of the family and sat at their table nightly for dinner. Six more months went by and Vito received tragic news from his Brother-in-law in Cleveland that his Sister Maria had passed away during childbirth and that Vito had a Nephew, Michael. Vito was distraught by the news and went to Cleveland to be with his Brother-in-law at his time of need.

Vito returned to the farm after spending two weeks with his brother-in-law and newborn nephew Mikey. To get over his loss of his sister he became fully engrossed in his work. For several weeks Vito spent many extra hours in the field, long after the workers had left for home. One evening Mr. Roberto walked out to the field and approached Vito.

"Vito! I know that you are going through a difficult time now. The loss of a loved one makes you want to be alone with your own thoughts. But Vito what you need now is people around you that can help you through this period in your life. I want you to spend more time with us."

"I think that you are right Mr. Roberto."

"Come! Let's go back to the house. My wife has fixed a huge bowl of pasta for us this evening. That and a nice glass of wine will make you feel better."

Mr. Roberto's friendship was invaluable in helping Vito get through his period of mourning. Things began to smoothly fall back into place.

In Vito's third year on the farm, Mr. Roberto passed away leaving Mrs. Roberto and two children with the large farm and no one to run it. Vito volunteered to operate the farm for the family who had been so good to him. But Mrs. Roberto had no desire to continue farming. She put the farm up for sale. It took eight months for them to get a buyer and Vito worked the farm until it was sold. The new owner asked him if he would like to stay on and run the farm for him. Vito refused and returned to Cleveland and his Brother-in law.

After several weeks of unsuccessfully looking for work Vito ran into an acquaintance living on the East side.

"Ciao Sam!" said Vito.

"Ciao Vito! How are you doing my friend? Are you still working on the farm?"

"No! The owner died and the family sold the business. The new owner asked me to stay but I couldn't. I've been out of a job for five weeks now and I have to find something or else I can't pay the bills."

"I'm out of work too Vito. But I heard that The

Ford Motor Company, you know Henry Ford up in Detroit, well he is hiring workers to help him build automobiles."

"Maybe we should go there and get a job!"

"Yes! Maybe we should. When would you be ready to leave Cleveland?"

"Well I have a few things to take care of first. But I think that by early next week I will be ready." said Vito.

"What do you have to do that you need so much time? Are you married now?"

"No but I have a brother-in-law and a nephew that I have to make sure that they are alright. Then I have to give notice to the Land Lady. I can't just up and leave. I do have some responsibilities."

"You are right. I have my family too, so I need a little time too. What if we leave on Tuesday of next week?"

Yes! That is OK for me."

"OK Vito! We will leave Tuesday morning at eight o'clock."

"Ciao Sam!"

"Ciao Vito!"

Reluctantly, not knowing anything about automobiles, Vito decided to move there with his acquaintance in late 1924.

They traveled by rail from Cleveland to Detroit.

The automobile industry was booming when they

arrived and work was to be had by anyone willing to work. Vito and his friend Sam worked on the automobile assembly line. It did not take long to learn to install the same few parts on the automobile that Ford were producing. It was constant repetition and monotonous. However the pay was good. As a bonus the Ford Company allowed its employees to purchase new cars at a sizable discount. Vito had a new car every year while employed by Ford. In 1927, Vito became a naturalized citizen of the United States of America. This was his proudest moment. He and his friend along with two women that they were dating went out on the town to celebrate.

In early 1929 after almost four years with the company the boom ended. Vito and his friend were out of work.

"Vito! I heard that the City of Detroit is hiring for their Transportation Department. Let's go see if they have a job for us?"

They looked for work with the City of Detroit. Both were given jobs in the Transportation Department. Their job was to maintain the central trolley power facility. The Trolley was operated by under ground wire cable that was a loop that originated at the central facility and ran constantly below the streets that were serviced by the trolley. For a trolley to move it would lock on to the cable and thus move to the next passenger loading point.

After working for the City of Detroit for almost one year in January of 1930 the City decided to upgrade their transportation system and began phasing out the cable cars and installing electric wires above the tracks to power the motorized trolley cars. Needless to say, they both lost their jobs. They were promised however that they would be rehired as soon as things settled and the new city budget was approved.

They decided that they would stay on in Detroit for as long as they could. Both had set aside some money in case of future need. Vito had come to like Detroit and was in no hurry to move elsewhere. He loved to dance and there were places that had orchestras on Fridays, Saturdays and Sundays. He spent his weekends enjoying himself meeting young ladies on the dance floor.

The two friends hung on in Detroit for two months waiting for the new city budget to get them back to work. During this time they searched for temporary work. Things did not look good in the job market. It was difficult to find work during this period. The great depression of 1929 had devastated the economy. They were idle for two months living from the money that they had set aside. However as things go, at the end of the two months they found out that the city budget had been severely cut and no new jobs were available.

Vito's friend had proven to be a real find. He was in contact with relatives that lived in Ohio.

"My cousin and his family live in a small town in Ohio. He wrote to me about work in the Brickyard there and also a plant that made fifty-five gallon barrels was hiring. What do you think Vito! Do you want to move there with me? At least maybe we can get some work and make some money. What do you think?"

"Well that sounds alright to me Sam. Is it near Cleveland?"

"Not too far from there. Maybe we can get a room together until we make some money. My cousin told me that he would look for a place for us to live so that if we decide to go there we will have a place to live. Shall I write and tell him we're coming?"

"Yes! Let's go because I don't think that we are going to get any work here!"

"OK! I will send him a letter!"

In March of 1930 they came to the small town, and began applying for a job. They both worked temporarily for the Brickyard making fired brick for the roads that were being paved in the area. Later as work ran out Vito applied for a job at the Barrel Works and was hired. Sam got a job in the New Castle, Pennsylvania area and moved to be close to his job.

The Mason Woods

Chapter 3

Immigration of Isabella

Isabella resides in the village of Tursi in the County of Matera Italy. Her mother Maria was born and raised here. Isabella and her two brothers and two sisters know only this village. Growing up in Tursi they have many friends and relatives that are going to be left behind. The family's relatives are merchants and have two establishments in the small commercial area. The land immediately surrounding Tursi has an abundance of fruits and olive trees. The olive oil that is produced in Tursi is stored in caverns that are dug into the sides of the surrounding mountains. Olive oil has been stored this way in Tursi for centuries. There are approximately three thousand citizens living in the village.

The remains of a castle known as the Burgh of Rabatana overlooks the village of Tursi. The Ostrogoths built the castle in the 5th century. The

Ostrogoths (Greuthung, Gleaming Goths or Eastern Goths), along with the Visigoths (Noble Goths or Western Goths) were branches of the Goths, an East Germanic tribe that played a major role in the political events of the late Roman Empire.

In the 9th century Tursi was a stronghold of the Saracens in southern Italy. There are two churches in Tursi the church of St. Mary of Anglona, which sits at the top of the hill and visible from all parts of the village. It was built in the 12th century. A second church is the church of Santa Maria Maggiore (10th-11th centuries).

Isabella and her family said their goodbyes to their friends and neighbors. Many tears were shed. Frank and Grace were the youngest and had to be pulled out of school. Their classmates, wanted to leave with them to go to the United States. There was much apprehension. They were leaving their close family and friends of many years for a trip to a place they knew nothing about but had heard from their Father that it was a great place to raise a family and opportunities are unlimited. He promised that all would be well once they arrived. (John Batiste) Isabella's Father came to the United States in 1923. John was sponsored to come to the United States by a relative in Las Vegas, NV.

Upon arrival in The United States he boarded a railroad train that brought him to his sponsor in Nevada. After spending several weeks with the family he left Las Vegas and proceeded to San Francisco. After searching for several weeks, with the help of friendly Italians, John found a job in San

Francisco as a Porter on the Union Pacific Railroad. The constant cross country traveling provided him with a good view and feel for The United States. John enjoyed his work and after five and one half years of traveling across the country John settled in the small city in Ohio.

Having learned English while working as a Porter he was able to communicate with the locals. John found work at a local mill called the Falcon Foundry. The Catholic Church was preparing to tear down its Rectory and replace it with a new stone building. To establish roots for himself and his family John purchased the rectory of St. Stephens Church and had it transported to the East side of town. John had purchased a lot and had a basement dug and a foundation built to set the rectory upon. He had saved his money to pay for his families' passage from Italy to the U.S.A.

Isabella arrived in New York City in September of 1929 with her Mother Mary, two Brothers Anthony (Tony), Frank (Chi-Chi) and two Sisters Rose and Grace. John went to Ellis Island to pick up his family. They were greeted and embraced by their father and husband (John Batiste). Many tears of joy were shed since they had not seen each other's for almost seven years. He was pleasantly surprised at how his children had grown since he last saw them. Isabella was elated to see her Father and Mother joined together once more. They were both very happy. They were a family reunited in their new homeland The United States of America. They went to Grand Central Station where they boarded a train that would take them to the small city, their new home.

The family came to the small city, on the edge of the Mason Woods. Isabella and her family did not speak a word of English. Within two weeks as they were beginning to become accustomed to each other tragedy struck. John, her father, caught pneumonia and passed away. The family was in turmoil. There was no one they could turn to for help. During the funeral they meet many Italian neighbors who offered their condolences as well as offering any help they could give them in this time of need.

The Pastor of the Mount Carmel Catholic Church, Father Santoro took them under his wing and helped in whatever way he could. He introduced them to a prominent lawyer who spoke Italian, James Lapolla, esq.. Mr. Lapolla helped them with any documents that were required. His family became friends of Isabella and her family. One of the Lapolla family members came by regularly to make sure that the family had all the necessities.

The family was in dire straits. Very little money and no one to turn to for help. None spoke English. They did not know the lay of the land. They relied on other Italian neighbors who spoke English to help them with their basic needs. It was a very difficult and trying time for them. Father Santoro approached the wealthier members of his church asking them to provide support for the family in need. With Isabella's expertise in the kitchen and the contributions of food from the neighbors, their first Epiphany (Italians do not celebrate Christmas as we know it) in the United States was a sad one because of the loss of their Father. However there was food on the table. They had each other. They were warm and they were safe.

And so was their beginning in their new land.

In 1930 Anthony, being nineteen years old and the oldest Son became the acting Father of the family. He contacted Italian neighbors and got instructions on what he could do for the family to help them through this crisis. They were translators as well as friends.

A neighbor who worked for a local Steel Mill suggested that maybe he could help Anthony get a job at the Steel Mill. Anthony agreed that if he could find work, the family would be able to provide for themselves. With the help of the neighbor the local Steel Mill employed Anthony. He provided the income needed for the survival of his family. Anthony worked for this Steel Mill until he retired at the age of sixty-five. Ever grateful for the help the Steel Mill provided in his time of need.

The family was now stable. They were finally independent. Capable of sustaining themselves. They were learning the ways of life in the United States. They thanked God every day for removing them from the peasantry of Southern Italy.

The Mason Woods
Chapter 4
Two Immigrants Meet

The owner of the apartment that Vito and his friend Sam had been sharing was above a corner grocery store called Ann Street Groceries on the East side of the small city. The store serviced a small area of the East side. They specialized mainly in Italian products since the majority of the residents on the East side were Italian. One day as Vito was shopping in the grocery store the owner Mrs. Rizzi told him about the family that lived three blocks away.

"Vito! Come over here I want to talk to you!"

Groceries in hand Vito walked toward the cash register where Mrs. Rizzi was standing.

"Vito! I want to ask you something. How old are you?"

"I am twenty-nine years old. Why do you ask?"

"Well! Did you ever think about settling down and raising a family? "

"I'm too busy trying to make a living! Right now

47

I don't have time for a girl friend."

"There is a family that just came from Italy, from Tursi. They are here for two weeks and the Father died. None of them speaks English and they need help! There is a nice daughter that you should meet. She would be just right for you! Go and visit them! I'm sure they would like to meet you!"

"Mrs. Rizzi! For you I will do this favor."

Vito paid for his groceries and went up to his apartment. That afternoon all dressed up in a three piece dark blue pin stripe suit, red tie, black patent leather shoes and a light grey fedora he went into the grocery store.

"Oh Vito! I have never seen a gentleman as good looking as you. If I wasn't married and thirty years younger, I would chase after you myself."

Vito smiled. He gathered a batch of groceries and brought them to the counter. Mrs. Rizzi bagged the groceries filling two bags. He paid and then proceeded to walk bags in hand to the house of the newly arrived family. It was a distance of three blocks to the house. His thoughts were about what he would say to the family.

Upon arrival, he set one bag down on the front porch and rapped on the door. A young man answered the door.

"Good Afternoon! My name is Vito. I wish to offer my condolences on the loss of your Father"

"Thank you! My name is Frank but everyone calls

me Chi Chi. Come in please!"

Chi Chi took the bags of groceries and he and Vito, hat in hand, entered the house.

"Mama! I would like you to meet Vito."

Taking her hand "Choa Signora! I wish to offer my condolences on the loss of your husband. What was his name?"

"His name was John!"

"Where does the family come from?"

"We come from a small town called Tursi a principality of Matera. We got here about a month ago and my husband died from pneumonia two weeks ago. Thank you very much for your gift! This is my oldest daughter Isabella!"

Vito took her hand in both hands and gazed into her eyes.

"A pleasure to meet you Isabella! I offer my condolences on the loss of your Father."

"Thank you for that and thank you very much for the gift that you brought."

Vito offered his condolences to each as he was introduced. Saying a few kind words as he shook each ones hand. There was a spark between Vito and Isabella when he took her hand in both of his hands and offered his condolences. The family graciously accepted his condolences and his generous gifts.

Isabella enamored Vito. The handsome gentleman who stood before her swept Isabella off her feet.

Resplendent in his appearance and manners. The family related the ordeal that they had gone through with the passing of their Father and Husband. They asked if he would like to stay and have a cup of coffee and some cookies that Isabella had baked. He accepted. The conversation encompassed the voyage and their seeing the Statue of Liberty. Going through Ellis Island was a bit hectic due to not speaking English, however, they made it through. Vito complemented Isabella on her baking abilities.

When the visit was over and Vito left, Isabella told her Mother that she was going to marry that man. Vito became a regular visitor at Isabella's house for the next few months. His knowledge of the English language was a great help to the family during this time. Isabella was impressed. After a courtship of about one year, in January 1931, Vito proposed to Isabella and they got married. Vito said that he spent his last six hundred dollars towards buying Isabella's wedding dress and the wedding reception. But he said it was worth every penny. On February 29, 1932, I was born. Phillip.

During my first few years, Dad struggled to put food on the table. Jobs were very hard to find. After my first birthday, Dad received word from his Aunt in Arnold Pennsylvania that Pittsburgh Plate Glass was looking for workers. Mom and Dad packed everything, which was not much, and we traveled to Pittsburgh. Dad got a job and we found a place to live that was close to his Aunt Francis's home. After six weeks there was a layoff in which Dad was included. He then heard that the West Virginia coalmines were hiring so he went to West Virginia alone and left Mom and I alone. Fortunately we were close to his Aunts home. Mom had someone she could turn to for companionship. Two weeks later Dad returned. The coalmines were not for him. Coal mining is not a job for someone who enjoys the outdoors and likes to work with the soil. We packed up and returned to the small city in Ohio, to be near the rest of the family.

On August 19, 1933, my brother Johnny was born. Dad worked several jobs during the next few years but never one that he was able to hang onto. The famous depression had taken hold.

The Mason Woods
Chapter 5
Hard Times

As youngsters, Johnny and I didn't notice that the economy was bad and that there were no jobs for people to earn money to put food on the table. We ate. We played with the other children in the neighborhood and all was well.

Neighbors leave their doors open overnight without fear. In this period between the Big Depression and World War II, the majority of the people have nothing. There is no wealth to speak of. Most have their homes and very few have an automobile. Most live from week to week with the wage that they earn. Some who are in need receive welfare. Picking up necessities at the city center consisting of dried legumes of various sorts, flour, rice, dried apricots, dried prunes and raisins. I normally took my little beat up red wagon and walked to town with Dad each week to pick-up our rations. Along with the dried foods, you are also given a coupon worth five dollars that you take to the local market and purchase various cuts of meats. For five dollars you can purchase approximately twenty pounds of the more expensive cuts of meat. Hamburger is ten cents a pound. Round steak was fifteen cents a pound. Bologna was five cents a pound. A loaf of Wonder Bread is a Nickel. The people have much respect for one another during this time. They have a common goal. Survival.

This is a time when lighter than air ships fly through the air going from their hangers in Akron to their destination, usually Cleveland. The most famous of the airships is the German Zeppelin the Hindenberg. It was built and used to fly passengers around the world. The gas that filled the ship was hydrogen. A highly volatile, explosive gas. The United States used Helium in their air ships to provide the lift. It was a stable gas that would not ignite and therefore the safer of the two gases. The Hindenburg eventually met its fiery doom while hovering to land in Lakehurst, New Jersey in 1939. We heard the broadcast on the radio. The newsreels in the movie theater showed the disaster.

The vision of the huge monsters, gliding, engines roaring, is an amazing site to behold. You first notice them when you hear the sound of their engines off in the distance. They then slowly come into view. They move as if going through water. Just as a ship at sea whose bow rises and then falls and rolls from side to side. They are usually in sight for a full twenty minutes from horizon to horizon. When out of sight, you can still hear the engines.

We have a friend who is retarded. He is three years older than I. He is strong as a bull. Has never spent a day in school as far as I know. If you have anything heavy to lift, he is your man. His name is Philip. As we watched an air ship passing overhead, we coaxed him to knock it down with a stone.

"Philip! Knock down the blimp! Said Johnny.

He obligingly found a large stone the size of his fist and with all his strength, hurled it towards the air ship, which was a few thousand feet in the air. The stone almost vanished from sight. Then he stood there grinning from ear to ear. All his teeth showing. He was looking for approval from us, which was generously given.

"Wow! That was great Philip! Wow! You almost knocked it down!" patting him on the back.

Philip never asks to participate in any games. He is satisfied to stand and watch. Arms limp at his side. Philip has one eyebrow that goes from his right temple to his left temple. When he runs or walks, his arms never swing away from his sides. They are always stationary. This makes him standout when he is running. When you look into his eyes, they seem to be spinning. No one ever says a cross word to Philip. No one dares.

One day we were asked to join a group of guys our own age for a football game on an empty lot on Scott St. Next to a grocery store. No one owned a real football. We usually took a newspaper and folded and rolled it until it formed a rounded shape, took Mason jar rubbers, and wrapped them around the formed ball until they were tight. This was our football.

After throwing our makeshift ball around a few times, we decided to choose sides and start our game. As we played, a seventeen year-old named Guy, whose mother owned the grocery store, decided to come over and interfere with our game by jumping in and stealing the football away from us and taunting us.

"Give back the football!" said one of our friends.

"Make me! Said Guy. "Come and take it away from me if you think you can!!

"Guy! Give us back our football. We want to play our game," said Johnny.

"Who do you think you are stupid! If you don't shut up I'll shove these newspapers down your throat! You don't belong on this street anyway! Why don't you go back over on your street where you belong and take your brother with you!"

"Guy! Give us back our ball and leave us alone!" We want to continue with our game!" I said.

"Do you think you can take it? You sissy! You and your brother are nothing but a bunch of sissies! And you're the biggest sissy!"

He began picking on me. I went up to him.

"Give me the football!"

Guy was much taller then I. When I stood up to him my eyes were level with his chest.

"If you want this football you will have to take it

away from me!" he challenged.

As he began to yell at me, I kicked Guy in the shins and when he bent down to my size I punched him in the mouth. Guy began to cry and ran home. Two minutes later his mother came over and began yelling at us for hitting her son. We ignored her for a short time.

"Mrs. C.! Your son came over and bothered us! He started it by stealing our football! We're younger than him and he should go play with kids his own age and leave us alone!"

"You are hoodlums, you and your brother! When I see your mother I'm going to tell her how bad you two are!" she yelled.

She left. As many times as we played football in that open lot Guy never came over to see what was going on.

The Mason Woods

Chapter 6

The Family

Mom excels in the peasant style of cooking of Southern Italy. She makes quite a variety of pasta by hand. Mom also bakes fresh bread for us every fourth day. Occasionally she would make her delicious pizza. In Southern Italy, the peasants make very few meals using meat. Thus our meals were usually with a mixture of pasta and beans or pasta and greens of different sorts with some tomato sauce added.

A chicken was usually prepared for Sunday dinner. Mom made the chicken with oven roasted sliced potatoes or quartered caramelized sweet potatoes as the side dish. The white potatoes were roasted with garlic, onions and oregano. To me this was the best meal of the week. I basically live for Sunday dinner.

Since there is no refrigeration, on Saturday mornings, I went with Mom to a huckster who sold live chickens, ducks and pigeons out of his garage. The local grocery stores were also his clients. Mr. Raggazzo went to the farms every Thursday to gather up his birds. On Fridays and Saturdays he sold his live chickens and ducks for a nickel a pound. Pigeons, called squab, were sold for ten cents each.

Mom pointed to the chicken she wanted.

"Anthony! Give me that nice fat chicken." Mom said pointing at the flock"

Pointing with his five-foot long heavy wire shaped into a hook, Mr. Raggazzo asked.

"Is this the one you want?"

"Yes please weigh it for me!"

He snatched the chicken by one leg and then folded the wings under one another and placed the bird on the scale.

"This one weighs about five pounds Signora! I think that one over there is bigger. Do you want me to get that one?"

"Yes Please!" said Mom.

Weighing the next chicken he said, "This one is almost seven pounds. Do you want this one?"

"What is the price for it?"

"This one is thirty-five cents."

"OK Anthony I will take that one!"

He wrapped the chicken in newspaper and we brought it home.

Mom dressed the chicken with my watchful eyes

observing how she did this. The only thing that was wasted from the chicken were the feathers and the beak. The feet were scrubbed clean, peeled and used to make chicken soup. The blood was caught in a bowl, mixed with chopped onions and baked in the oven. The intestines were cut open, cleaned with running water, then soaked for a half hour in salt water, as were the feet the heart and the liver. These were added to the chicken soup along with rice. This was our Saturday evening meal. The chicken was roasted whole on Sunday with the neck and head still in place. The Sunday dinner is always either the traditional pasta and meatballs or the roasted chicken.

I loved to watch Mom cook. I stood next to the range and watched her create her magic.

She always teased me saying that some day I would become a cook. This made me feel proud although I knew that I was only interested in watching her cook, not to become a cook. Later she said that she really wanted me to become a teacher. I was not interested in that either, but I did not tell her.

On Saturdays and Sundays the family is at home. Family activities take precedence. Activities on the weekends consist of helping around the house with chores assigned by Mom and Dad. Dad has a beautiful garden that he takes pride in. The majority of the neighborhood is Italian and each family takes pride in being able to grow their own vegetables.

With Dads experience with plants no one could match his garden. He was a master and most would come to ask him for advice about specific plants that they were going to plant. Dad grew various vegetables but mainly tomatoes, which were canned in the fall to be used for cooking and peppers, which were strung up and hung in the basement for the winter.

There was always help needed to pull weeds. And sometimes Dad would let us hoe the ground around the plants with his close supervision. This did not happen very often because ten year olds do not have the control necessary to keep the blade of the hoe from striking down a plant. These activities usually took up the morning on Saturdays.

On Saturday afternoon Johnny and I walked to church for confession. To explain this process to those Non Catholics; In the Catholic Church one confesses any sins that he/she has committed since their last confession to a Priest. The Priest usually sits in a confessional, which is a booth with closed doors. The Priest sits in the middle stall while the people looking to confess their sins sit on either side of the Priest. After confessing your sins the Priest gives you absolution and a penance. The Penance consists of prayers to say after being forgiven by the Priest. The penance given is usually in direct correlation to the severity of the sins that you confess. Of course when you remain in the confessional a long while it usually means that you have more sins to confess.

Our church was one mile away from our home. In church, it is fun waiting for people to come out of the confessional to see who is in there the longest. When I go into the confessional, it never takes more than two or three minutes. I often wondered about those people who went in before us and stayed in the confessional for fifteen to twenty minutes. Then, they were still kneeling, doing penance, when we were leaving the church. What did they do to receive the wrath of the priest?

Occasionally the priest would raise his voice to someone in the confessional. We could not understand what he was saying but it was loud. We could not wait to see that person when the door to the confessional opened.

The Italian immigrants are very religious. They believe in going to church on Sunday and not eating meat on Fridays. During the school year, on Tuesdays and Fridays, Johnny and I went from grade school directly to the church basement for various church studies. The walk was a distance of one mile. Our instructor was a layperson Miss Lapolla a friend of our family.

She was nice and the children were all very attentive. The instruction usually lasted about an hour. By that time everyone was tired of sitting in the wooden folding chairs. The end of the session was welcomed.

One Friday after the study session was completed we lined up in the usual single file and came up the stairs that exit next to the rectory kitchen. The rectory is the Priests house. I could smell steak frying. As I got closer to the kitchen window I could actually hear the steak sizzling in the pan.

"Do you smell what I smell?" I asked Johnny.

"Yah! That smells like steak to me!"

"I thought we weren't allowed to eat meat on Fridays?"

"I know, but that smells and sounds like steak frying in a frying pan!" said Johnny.

Johnny and I arrived home. We sat at the dinner table. Mom had prepared spaghetti and green beans in tomato sauce. One of our typical Friday meals.

"Mom, we just came from church and the Priests' are having steak for dinner!"

"How do you know that Phillip, did you go inside their kitchen?"

"No Mom, but when we came from the basement we walked past the kitchen and Johnny and I could hear steak frying and the window was open and we could smell the meat!"

She shushed me holding her finger to her lips.

"Just eat!" she said.

On a certain Saturday, Mom and Dad had an appointment with the local photographer. Mom wanted a family portrait of the four of us. The photographer was located on the seventh floor of the tall bank building. The appointment meant it was time to get that dreaded haircut. Dad carried the stool into the front yard early in the morning. Then the usual fight broke out between Johnny and me. Neither of us wanted to be first. The tools for cutting hair are a comb, a scissors, a large towel and a hand

64

-operated clipper. The bad part of getting the haircut is that Dad is a very nervous person. And holding the clipper steady was impossible.

"Johnny! Why don't you go first!"

"I went first last time!"

"OK, I don't want to wait here while you two fight over who is first! Phil, get on the chair!" commanded Dad.

I sat down. Dad placed the towel around my neck and began to comb out my hair. He then took the hand clippers.

"Hold still now and don't move." Dad said.

Placing his hand on my head and holding the clippers in the other hand he began to cut away. Everything was going along fine until his hand tired from the squeezing motion needed to operate the hand clippers. Screams and tears became part of the ordeal. The more you screamed the more nervous Dad became.

"O.K. Phil! It wasn't that bad was it?"

I didn't respond. Johnny was next.

After the haircut Mom took us into the bathroom and washed us up. Early in the afternoon after lunch she dressed us in new white sailor suits with the dark blue trim on the collar flap and insignias on the sleeves. A new pair of shiny black-laced shoes made the outfit complete. The instructions were that we were going to leave for the photographer in two hours and we should keep clean and neat. We both agreed.

Yesterday, Johnny, Boo and I dug a small pit about eighteen inches in diameter and about a foot deep in the dirt pathway that people used to go to the corner store. Stash a friend from Baldwin Street was with us and offered to help.

"I'm going to get the pick out of the garage so we can dig faster. The shovel isn't good enough. I'll be right back," I said.

When I returned Stash was digging with the shovel.

"Give me the pick Phil!"

As Stash was putting the shovel aside he leaned towards the pick that I was holding. He hit the pointed end of the pick with his eyebrow. He started to spray blood from his head. We rushed to the water pump that was located in the back yard and washed his face off and cleaned out the wound. The cold well water stopped the bleeding.

"When I asked for the pick I didn't want you to hit me with it!"

"I'm sorry Stash! I didn't mean to hit you!"

Stash then left to go back to Baldwin Street. The task of digging the hole remained.

I returned the pick to the garage. We finished the hole using the spade. We then filled the hole with water and covered it so that no one would suspect that it was a trap.

The next day after getting dressed up for the photographer Johnny and I went to the trap. We found that the trap was still intact. No one had fallen in.

"I wonder if the cover is too tight?"

"Don't touch it Johnny! It looks OK to me!"

At that moment Johnny decided to test the trap with his foot. With his foot extended he leaned forward and fell into the trap splashing mud over both of us. Our new white sailor suits were covered in mud.

"Oh no! We're going to get it now!" I said.

Mom was keeping an eye on us from the kitchen window. I heard Mom screaming at the top of her lungs, running towards us. Needless to say we did not wear our navy suits to the photographer.

Sunday was the day for dressing up and walking to church. Johnny and I left the house at Eight Thirty to go to the Nine AM mass. As we walked along other children joined us on their way to Mass. Mass usually lasted for one hour. We did not like the early mass. But it did work out fine for the activities that took place later in the afternoon.

The Church Pastor Father Oreste always performed the Nine AM Mass. His sermons consisted mostly of needing to raise more money for the church. He usually became very animated and excited about the subject. It would turn to yelling and pointing to the ceiling for fifteen minutes. After the sermon was over I wondered how he regained control in order to continue with the Mass.

I usually could not wait for the Mass to end so that I could leave the Church. Although we never discussed it, I think that Johnny was also glad to leave the church. We were home by ten thirty. This gave us plenty of time to change and get ready for dinner. The Italian custom is to have your big mealfor lunch on Sundays. At least this was always the tradition in our house. This is probably a carry over from my parents' lives in Italy with their families. After lunch it was time to get ready to go to the theater.

The Mason Woods

Chapter 7

Our Close Friend

The school vacation begins in early June and lasts until Labor Day. Most days will be spent exploring the Mason Woods. On the last day of school students are usually home by 10:30 AM. That afternoon the neighborhood children gather to visit the Mason Woods.

Boo spends much of his summer vacation in the Mason Woods. Boo is eight. He is short and has a barrel like chest. A smile with dimples is permanently imprinted on his face. His brown hair is cut short. He has a fair complexion. A blue baseball cap was a permanent fixture on his head. Boo was friendly and easygoing. Always ready to pitch in or go along with whatever was happening. A true friend.

Boo has five Sisters and one Brother. He is child number six of the seven children. He got his nickname from his older brother Ralph. His given name is Thomas. Boos two favorite meals are the homemade ravioli or the lasagna that his mother prepares on Sundays.

Boos parents are Italian immigrants. Their knowledge of English is limited. They are basically good solid working people who are doing their best to raise their family. They had complete trust in Johnny and I to take care of Boo.

Boos Mom bakes home made bread in a small brick oven in the back yard. Everyone knows when she is baking bread. The aroma fills the neighborhood. Boos Father is a short rotund likable person. He works in one of the local manufacturing plants.

Boo is in the woods Monday through Friday during summer. You might say he lives in the woods with his two best friends, Johnny and I. We live on the same street. Johnny and I are older than Boo. Johnny is nine and I am ten.

The three of us meet at Eight AM and walk to Mason Woods together. After a day of fun and adventure we return promptly at four in the afternoon. Our orders are that you must be home when your father gets home from work. Dad would be home at 4:30, giving us time to become presentable when he arrived. It was rather difficult to achieve this goal with not having a wristwatch. However, the Four PM hour was never missed. Our empty stomachs saw to that.

The walk to Mason Woods takes half an hour, if there are no distractions. Usually we would carry a knife or small hatchet, sneaked from the garage.

After all, who knew what we might encounter in the woods. It is not unusual for others to ask to join us. There was plenty of fun and discovery to be had by all in the Mason Woods.

The Mason Woods

Chapter 8

Sundays

Early Sunday afternoon, the young people go to the movies. One must go to church on Sunday if one wants to go to the movies. The problems and mischief created during the week are forgiven on Sunday. The consensus is that If God can forgive you, so can your parents. Actually, it was that Mom having had her hands full all week is glad to have peace for half a day.

After attending mass we would have the special Sunday dinner that Mom prepared. Our main dinner on Sundays was at noon. Mom was not the best baker in the world however she did make the best lemon pie and the best banana cream that I have ever eaten. On this Sunday she surprised us with the best looking chocolate cake ever.

After the main course we each received a generous piece of chocolate cake and a large glass of milk. Mom and Dad of course had coffee. When we tasted the cake we did not know what to say.

Dad then said "Why is this cake so tasty!"

Mom had yet to taste the chocolate cake.

When she did she stated, "Don't tell me that I used salt instead of sugar! Oh my God!"

We all began to laugh, lovingly at Mom's error. She of course joined us.

"Don't eat the cake." said Mom. "I will throw it out."

Johnnie and I continued to eat the cake until it was gone.

"Don't throw it out Mom. It tastes really good!" said Johnnie.

"I think so too, Mom!"

"Just leave it Isabella. We'll eat it."

Mom laughed. "If you like it, OK."

Our parents gave each of us fifteen cents. A dime for the theater and a nickel for a treat. Usually rain, shine, sleet or snow all the children in the neighborhood go to the movies. I cannot remember one time that anyone was missing. Well, there was the one time that Salvatore had the mumps and was quarantined for two weeks. The moviegoers meet at the same time and place in the neighborhood. We then walk as a group to town a distance of two miles. Eagerly anticipating the entertainment.

"Can't wait to see what happened to the hero. I'll bet that he makes it!" I said.

"That's impossible! That fast moving train hit the car and he was in it! Said Boo.

"Well! If he got killed, then the serial is over. They'll announce it in this weeks serial. If they do you know what that means. It means that the spies won!" said Johnny.

"I think that he'll jump out before the train hits!" said Sal.

"They showed the car with him in it when the train hit. He was still in the front seat!" said Johnny.

"Well, we're just going to have to wait and see!" I said.

"Did you guys hear the boxing match on the radio Friday night?" asked Sal.

"I didn't! Did anyone else?" I asked.

No one had listened in.

"Man it was a good fight! It went for eight rounds and then Willie Pep knocked him out!"

"Who did he fight Sal?" I asked.

"Joey Iannotti! He put up a good fight but Willie Pep was too much for him."

There are three movie theaters, in town. The theater that is most popular for the young crowd is, the Warner Theater. On Sunday afternoons, it is usually packed with young people age seven to twelve. It is

75

said that this theater is the original. The first Warner Theater, before the Warner Bros. name became famous. We later learned that the first Warner Theater built was in New Castle Pennsylvania in 1905. That was thirty-five miles away. Well, This Theater was very old, so it may have been the second Warner Bros. Theater. The doors open at 12:30 PM. The line of young people stretches around the corner, which is three storefronts away from the theater entrance. All impatiently waiting their turn to come up to the booth and pay Veronica their dime. Veronica is an elderly lady that has worked the ticket booth at the Warner for as long as I can remember. Occasionally looking over her shoulder is Sid the manager. Sid is Lebanese. He is a friendly soul. He is roughly thirty-five years old, wears glasses, partially bald, round in stature and always dressed in a suit and tie. Sid always smelled good. He never fails to say a kind word to his young customers. The movie houses all charge a dime for their Sunday Matinee. But the Warner Theater gives you more for your money.

Upon entering, the aroma of fresh popcorn exploding fills the air of the small lobby. Popcorn or candy can be purchased for a nickel. You usually passed on this so that your nickel could be better used to purchase a comic book at the drug store, after the entertainment. The carpeting in the dimly lit walkway beyond the lobby is well worn. The bare floor in the seating aisles is sticky from the spilling of soft drinks over the years. The seats have seen better days. They are almost uncomfortable to sit in.

But the young crowd does not mind. We are here for the entertainment. Anyway, the owners probably felt that since everything takes place in the dark, no one will notice.

The Sunday program begins at 1:00 PM. The theater is filled to capacity with noisy screaming young people. The noise ends with a loud cheer as the lights are dimmed and then go out. The program begins with the first movie usually a western then followed by a Disney cartoon. Then came the long awaited serial.

We all sat on the edge of our seats. Watching intently. It was so quiet that you could hear everyone's heart pounding. The serial began before the car/train crash so that everyone would be brought up to speed on the serial.

"Here it comes!" said Johnny.

We all watched with anticipation as the scene of the crash showed that the hero escaped just prior to the crash.

The theater shook from the roar of the youngsters.

"I told you!" said Sal laughingly.

"What a bunch of phonies! I can't believe that they would do something like that. They fooled us!" said Boo.

"I think we knew he wouldn't be killed! We just didn't want to admit it. This serial will end when the hero catches the spy ring." I said.

The Movie Tone News showed scenes of the war that was going on in Europe, which none of us were interested in. Then comes the second movie. The second movie is also a western. But for children in our age group this is excitement to see the cowboys and the horses. The noise in the theater peaks and wanes as the program continues. There are shouts and yells when a bad man, the man in the dark hat, is preparing to shoot the good man, the man in the white hat. The cheers when the good man wins the battle are so loud that you have to cup your hands over your ears. It comes to an end at 5:30 PM. A full four and one half hours of entertainment.

The walk home takes us through Central Park. There is a lively exchange of comments about the various characters and plots in the theater program. There are always arguments over who said what in the films as well as disagreement over what is going to happen next to the hero in the serial. Is he going to live for the next chapter? Or how is he going to get out of the mess he got into?

Then comes the usual stop at the drugstore to buy a comic book. The owner of the drugstore is happy to see us, but is happier when we leave. A group of hyper children who mess up his comic book rack. Leafing through all the comic books to find the one they want. Comic books are not wrapped in a protective covering.

We then line up at the counter to pay for our treasures. We all then walk home with our comic book in hand. Still discussing the afternoon's entertainment.

Mom usually has prepared a chicken, oven roasted

with a mixture of white and sweet potatoes for supper. We could smell the chicken from a block away. Supper is always ready when Johnny and I come in the door. She knew exactly to the minute when we would arrive. And she knew that we would be hungry. Mom has this knack for caramelizing the potatoes perfectly in the roasting pan. Some would stick to the sides of the pan and had to be scrapped to remove them to the serving platter. These were the best. The four of us sat down to a delicious meal with plenty for each of us. Life was good.

The Mason Woods
Chapter 9
Games We Played

Our neighborhood was made up of many empty lots. Each side of the street on our block between the cross streets at both ends had 16 lots. On our side of the street were nine empty lots. Across the street there were only a total of four houses. This left a large opening between the houses, which we used as a baseball field. The Parks and Recreation Department, headed by a man called Bill, would come several times a year and scrape the infield of the baseball diamond. A huge tractor was used to do this. Although the field did not belong to the City Parks Department, the maintenance was done since many youngsters used the empty lots as a ball field. At times we would see the barber out on the field hitting golf balls. The field was the gathering place for young people from a large part of the East Side of town.

"Johnny do you remember that Andy said we could borrow his golf clubs?"

"Yah Phil, I remember. Do you want to go hit some balls?"

"I'm for that! Let's go hit some balls!" said Boo.

"Did you ever hit a golf ball Boo?"

"No, but it might be fun!"

"OK, let's go to Andy's house! This might be fun!" exclaimed Johnny.

Andy was 17 years old and lived on our block. Andy loved to get out on the big field and hit golf balls. He could really hit the ball a long way.

I knocked on his door. We waited patiently for the door to open..

"Hi guys!".

"Hi Andy!" we responded. "We would like to borrow your golf clubs and a couple of balls." I said.

"Sure! Let me get them. I'll be right back!"

Andy came out with three clubs and three balls..

"Have some fun and don't break any windows. When you hit the golf ball, it will go a long way. So, be careful. If I'm not here when you are done just leave the stuff on the front porch near the door."

"Thank you Andy."

We walked to the baseball field. We each put a ball down and prepared to hit the ball.

"Let's see who can hit the ball farthest!" said Boo.

"OK, Let me go first," I said.

"Here goes!"

The ball bounced over the field only to land about thirty feet away.

"Can I go next?" asked Boo! .

"Hit a hundred yarder!"

After three swings and misses, he hit the ball in the air for a short distance.

"Good one Boo!"

Johnny stepped up to the ball and with one swing lifted the ball in the air and the ball went past both our balls.

"Nice shot! I know you never held a golf club before, but you hit the ball like a pro," I said.

We walked towards the balls. In the order of closest to farthest away we proceeded to hit the balls around the field. After one hour of this we agreed that golf was not our thing. Chasing after a little ball was not exciting for youngsters our age.

We placed the clubs over our shoulders and began our trek over the field towards the neighbor's house to return the equipment.

Boo said "I see old John with his hat on looking for baseballs in his garden."

Johnny swung around to view Old John and slammed the iron part of the golf club into my right eyebrow. Blood gushed down across my face.

"Jesus John, watch what your doing!"

As he turned back to the other side, he narrowly

missed clipping Boo.

"Get the club off your shoulder before you get me again!"

"I didn't mean to hit you!"

"I know you didn't but carry the club in your hand so you don't hit someone else!"

I went home to clean up while Johnny and Boo returned the clubs to Andy. I sneaked in through the back door and went down to the basement to wash up. I stopped the bleeding by pressing a cold wet cloth to my brow. Fortunately, after it stopped bleeding, it was hardly visible under the hair of my right eyebrow. Mom and Dad never found out.

The baseball field was the center of activity for our extended neighborhood. There was always a group of guys playing baseball. When someone came to the field, he could ask to join the game that was in progress. If there was a full complement of players, eighteen, then the person could ask to get in on the next opening. Guys were always coming and going. The age range of the players was from ten years old to twenty-four years old. Mostly they were in the ten to 16 year range.

There were no fences on the baseball field. Down the third baseline, two hundred and seventy five feet away was the street. The first baseline had no restrictions. Forty feet adjacent to the third base line was a well-maintained fenced garden. It ran along the third base line to the street. When there was a game going on Old John a boarder at the house would stand in the center of the garden waiting for foul balls to be hit into the garden. A boarder is a person who is renting a room from an owner and is also provided his daily meals. John would stand out in the garden for hours with his brown bowler on his head. When a foul ball went into the garden, the game was over. John would run for the ball and then run into the house with our ball in hand. There would be jeering and name-calling until John was in the house. Then we would all pickup our belongings and head for home.

Baseballs and bats are expensive items. I never owned one. I do not know where the balls and bats we used came from. It seems there was never more than one ball and seldom were there two bats. Someone was always willing to lend you a glove if they had one.

A group of boys that lived closer to the Mason Woods constructed a framed hut approximately one hundred yards behind home plate. They worked on the hut for several weeks undisturbed. They would bring in planks of wood and roofing materials from home or elsewhere. They would saw and nail until it was completed.

On a day that there was no one working on the hut Johnny, Boo and I decided to walk over and investigate. We made sure that none of the boys were within sight.

"It looks like they did a good job. But it won't hold out the rain," I said.

"I just walked around it and there is no door," said

Boo.

"Let's take a closer look," said Johnny.

We slowly walked around the hut twice checking for any sign of an entry.

"There is no door! The next time they come around we have to see how they get in," I said.

We returned to the ball field.

As we played ball, we kept an eye on the hut. In a while Boo spotted two of the guys who had been working on the hut. They went behind the hut and were seen no more. They disappeared for an hour. They then reappeared and walked towards where they lived. When they were out of site, Johnny, Boo and I walked over to the back of the hut.

"I don't know how they got in. It had to be at the back of the hut. There has to be an entrance," I said.

We searched the back wall for ways to enter but none could be found. I began to search the ground beyond the wall.

"Here it is! See the drying piece of sod! That's where it's at," I said.

Underneath the patch of grass was a wide board. I lifted the board. It revealed a tunnel, just wide enough for a small person to squeeze through. I glanced around to see if anyone was looking.

"Let's go in to see what it looks like! Boo you go first and then you go Johnny."

The length of the tunnel was approximately fifteen feet.

"Are you in there yet Boo?"

"Just about there Phil!"

"OK! Johnny is in the tunnel and I'm coming in now."

Entering the hut I could see that they had done a good job. The hut was solid. We did not disturb anything. We did not want the owners to know that someone had entered their hut. We went back through the tunnel. We made sure that the board and grass were left as we found them.

Three blocks South of our house where the street ended were the railroad tracks. The tracks were about twenty feet below the level of the land on both sides of it. The railroad engines that used the tracks are steam driven and coal fired. This resulted in billowing clouds of black smoke filling the air as the trains huffed and puffed pulling their string of cars toward their destination. When we had a couple of pennies, which was rare, we walked down to the railroad tracks and would place the pennies on one of the rails and then climb up the bank to wait for a train to come by to mash the pennies.

A game we played as we waited was to leap from the top of the bank to see who would land farthest away from the jump off point. The bank consisted of very soft dirt so it was safe to land on after a leap. We would stand back about fifteen feet from the edge of the bank. Then we would run as fast as possible towards the edge and launch into the air as far and high as possible. Arms flailing in the air to maintain your balance.

"I'm going to go first this time!"

I ran forward as fast as my legs would carry me and jumped as high and as far out over the bank as I could. I landed in the soft sandy soil, my shoes leaving imprints in the sand where I landed.

"I can't jump that far!" said Boo.

"Try to do your best. Run real fast then jump like your trying to reach the sky."

"OK, here I go!"

Boo ran as fast as his short legs could go. When he came to the edge he couldn't give much of a push. He landed with his feet in the soil about half way down the slope.

"See, I told you that I couldn't do any good!"

"Boo, that isn't bad! After all you're shorter than us. You'll do better next time. Try harder and see if you can go past your last marks."

"OK Johnny! Your turn!"

Johnny didn't need any coaching. He ran to the edge, leaped out and landed almost as far as my tracks.

"Good jump brother!"

We would then smooth the area so that the footprints disappeared and resumed with a new set of leaps.

This game continued until we heard the shrill whistle of the oncoming steam engine.

"Lets go back up the hill so we can watch the steam engine run over the pennies." I said.

We then climbed to the top of the bank and sat. Eyes glued on the pennies. As the train rolled over the

88

coins they disappeared after the second or third wheel rolled over them. After the train passed we went down to the rail to see if we could find the flattened pennies. No longer being on the rail, we searched along the side of the rail for fifteen to twenty feet. As many times as we placed pennies on the rails, we never found one of them after they had been smashed.

After supper the neighborhood youngsters would gather under one of the street lights in the middle of the block to play games such as Tag, Hide and Seek or a game which was known to us as Kick the Can. Kick the Can involved splitting the group into two teams. One team would guard the can placed in the middle of the roadway. This was called the Jail. The second team would hide anywhere within the limits that were established. Sometimes the limits would be an area covering three or four parallel streets. The object of the game was for the jailers to seek out the ones hiding, capture them and bring them to the can. One or two people then guarded them. For those hiding, it was their responsibility to overwhelm the guards and kick the can releasing those that are jailed. The game ended when the jail was filled and there was no one left to capture, or we were tired of playing. Usually it was the latter.

One day we were challenged by group of boys from a nearby neighborhood. Several of us accepted the challenge and went to meet the group that evening. In the heat of the game, one of our opponents, while chasing me, caught up to me and shoved me forward while I was running. I fell face first on to the street and scratched up my face and chipped one of my front teeth. I was in pain but I held back the tears.The game ended immediately. I was concerned about what my parents were going to say when we got home. I told Johnny that he was to say nothing to Mom and Dad. Mom found out immediately.

Sometimes we sat under the streetlight telling stories that we made up or had heard from friends. Some of these were scary or made to seem scary to excite the others. There was also discussion about the prizefighters that were popular. This always ended up in arguments over who was the best boxer in the various weight groups. Salvatore's two older brothers Leo and John Jr. were local boxers and therefore what Sal said the rest of us accepted.

Salvatore was a neighbor who lived on my side of the street. He was eight years old and his family consisted of one sister and four brothers. His older brothers Leo and John jr. were boxers. They boxed professionally at the local clubs in the general area like the VFW, The Elks or The Moose. Leo was the more successful, but never rose very high in the ranks of the professionals. The family had trucks and were in the hauling business.

Johnny and I had strict instructions that we must be home or on the way home at exactly nine o'clock. In a nearby smaller village, at nine o'clock every night an odd sounding siren would wail signifying that it was time for us to run home. The siren sounded more like the loud single short bellow of a bull. Dad would be waiting for us at the back door when we arrived.

One of my favorite things to do when the weather was bad was to go into our basement and work on a model airplane. I would spend hours cutting out the various parts stamped into the balsa wood using a razor blade. It was difficult to follow the lines. I would always have to glue parts together that were supposed to be cut out in one piece. This usually made the internal structure of the final product weak.

The models were powered by a rubber band. When I wound the propeller, the body would crunch up towards the propeller ruining my plane. But all was not lost. I would take my plane and a few matches and climb onto the garage roof. I would strike a match and set the body of the plane aflame. I would then launch it out over the grassy area. It gave me some satisfaction for all the hours that I put in to build it.

Model planes at this time cost five cents for the smaller ones and twenty-five cents for the larger deluxe models. My budget could only afford the five cents models.

The Mason Woods

Chapter 10

The Automobile Trip

The residential streets are mostly steamroller packed dirt. The need for paved side streets is not necessary. Only the main streets are paved with red firebrick that is manufactured locally.

The automobiles of the time are few and require as much maintenance time as time available for driving. An automobile trip is not measured by the number of miles, but by the number of flat tires or number of electrical problems you have. It is necessary to have a hand pump to inflate a tire, and a repair kit with patches and glue to fix a flat tire. For the electrical repair you have to go to a garage or a service station. It is only the daring that take long trips with their automobiles of ninety miles or travel at night.

I recall a trip to Arnold, PA to visit relatives. The

family was my Fathers Aunt on his Mothers side and the family that he came to when he first arrived in the United States. Arnold is ninety miles from our city.

On Friday morning at seven A.M. Dad stuck his head under the top hinged engine cover and did not come up for air until lunch time. Mom knew nothing about automobiles and Johnny and I were too young to know anything about anything, much less cars.

The lunch passed by with very few words other than Mom asking if everything was OK with the car. To which Dad replied in the affirmative. Whether that was the truth or not is debatable.

After lunch Dad went back to the car, so Johnny and I went to the baseball field to see if there was a game going on.

The field was a stones throw from our house. It was a large plot of land that took up eight vacant lots along the street that we lived on and more than eight lots on the next street. It was an area of approximately four hundred feet by four hundred feet plus. The field was also used by the local Catholic Church to hold their annual festival in August complete with fireworks. Attendance at the Church Festival was by people from our city as well as people from the neighboring cities.

As usual there was a game in progress. We both got a chance to play baseball. As mentioned previously the baseball field was situated next to a vegetable garden. Eventually, one of the players hit a long foul ball on the third base side. As usual, old John the mustachioed Serb/American waiting for the foul balls ran for the ball picked it up and then back into the house. Some of the players closest to the garden ran screaming at Old John to give back the ball. The game was over amidst screaming and cursing being leveled at Old John.

After three hours of playing ball sweaty and tired, we left the game to return home to see how things were going. Dad was closing the engine compartment and seemed to be satisfied that the car was ready to make the trip. Mom had prepared sandwiches to take with us so we had something to eat as we drove towards our destination the next morning. That night sleep came slowly. The anxiety of the long trip and what it held, plus meeting family that I do not remember meeting was on my mind.

We departed at 6:00 on Saturday morning, in my fathers 1932 Model A Ford. After about one hour on the road.

"When do you think we'll get there Dad?"I asked.

"We'll get there when we get there!" he answered.

"Leave your Father alone! Can't you see he's driving! Don't make him nervous!"

"OK Mom," I said.

Fifteen minutes later a tire went flat. Dad said something nasty in Italian and got out of the car.

"Get out of the car! I have to fix the flat tire!"

We all got out and Dad got the car jack and his repair kit and proceeded to go to work on jacking up the car. It was the right rear tire.

"Can I help you Dad?" I asked.

"No! Just stand over there out of the way so you won't get hurt!"

You could tell that Dad was upset. He probably did not think that he was going to have tire problems. But he was prepared for it. He had all the tools that he needed to make the repair.

After the patch had dried on the inner tube, Dad placed it into the tire and with his tire irons sealed the tire to the rim. He then pumped up the tire and placed it back on the axle. We all got in and away we went but not for long.

About forty-five minutes down the road there was a strange smell coming from the engine compartment. Dad started looking for a Service Station.

"What's wrong Dad?" asked Johnny.

"Vito, what is it now?"

"I don't know, but it smells like a wire is burning under the hood. We have to stop and let a mechanic look at it."

We pulled into the first Service Station that we could find. Dad got out of the car and went inside the station. They came out and the serviceman lifted the hood and started to look around. He and Dad talked for a short while and the man then went back to the garage and Dad came around to us.

"We have to wait! The serviceman said that the part that we need is in town and since today is Saturday, they might be closed so he may have to get the owner to open up to get the part. He said to come in and wait in the office."

We got out of the car and went into the Service Station office to wait. The chairs were not very comfortable to sit on, and there were only three chairs so Johnny and I took turns sitting. I could see that Mom wasn't very happy. I'm sure that Dad initiated this trip since he had not seen his Aunt for 8 years, and Mom was probably not too happy that she agreed to make the trip.

Two and one-half hours later, the part arrived. The owner of the Parts Store delivered the part since the store was closed on Saturdays. He apologized for taking so long, but he was at the church doing something and he didn't get the message till he got home. The serviceman and Dad went to the car while we waited in the office. Twenty minutes later Dad started the car and it seemed to be running fine.

Dad came in and said, "OK! Get into the car."

The three of us got into the car while Dad settled with the serviceman.

Mom didn't say a word, which was unusual for her. Dad got in the car and we were on our way once again.

About twenty minutes down the road a second tire went flat. This time it was the left front tire. I could see that Dad was furious. And Mom was really holding back. We got out of the car and Dad once again jacked up the car and proceeded to fix the flat. One hour later we were back on the road.

"Vito! Do you think we're going to make it? Or

should we turn back!"

With determination in his voice, Dad Said "Don't worry Isabella, we are going to make it!"

"I hope you are right. I don't want us to be stranded here in the middle of no where." You could sense the apprehension in Moms voice.

We arrived at our destination. It was three-thirty in the afternoon. Nine and one half hours to travel a distance of ninety miles. The car while running did well to go about thirty-five miles per hour. Well, it was faster then walking.

"Do you remember these streets Isabella?"

"They look familiar. But it has been a long time since we were here. They must live very close."

We drove up to this narrow two-story house. It stood on a hill along with other houses that filled the street on both sides. I had never seen houses built on the side of a hill before. The houses on the down hillside were lower than the street level and the houses on the up hillside of the street were above the street level. So to reach the houses on the down side of the hill, their driveway went down to the house. On the up hillside the driveway drove up to the house. This seemed very odd to me at the time, coming from the flat land of Ohio.

Mom said here we are kids. I hope Aunt Francis has made us something good to eat.

As we walked up to the front door Aunt Francis and Uncle Mike came hurriedly towards us. We all got hugs and kisses. Joyous conversation took place between my parents and Dads Aunt and Uncle as we entered the house. Dad was happy to see his Aunt and Uncle and two cousins whom he had not seen for several years. The initial discussion centered on the trip and the problems encountered. This lasted until dinner was served.

Since there were eight of us, and the dining table seated four, dinner was served in two shifts. The children were served first. There was not much conversation since my Fathers cousins were older and we really did not know them. The dinner consisted of a scrawny three-pound chicken and fried potatoes.

Mom, who was outspoken, said."Zia! The chicken is too small. How are we all going to eat from such a small bird! We are eight people!"

"We have enough! The kids don't eat much!" she stated.

"There are potatoes and a salad too."

After everyone had eaten we settled into the living room. Aunt Francis said that she would put on a pot of coffee, and went into the kitchen.

After half an hour had passed Mom asked,

"Zia! Are we going to have coffee?"

"Let me check if it is done."

Returning from the kitchen.

"It still has to go a little longer," she said.

After an hour passed by Mom asked her about the

coffee again. This time Mom went into the kitchen with her. I could hear Mom tell her that she had to put more coffee into the percolator. When the coffee was served Mom said that the coffee had no taste and no smell.

There were eight of us in the small two-bedroom house. The overnight stay was a disaster. The children shared the floor in the living room. Aunt Francis gave each of us a blanket and a pillow. We said our good nights and then the lights were turned out. I lay there thinking about the days happenings and all the effort put in by Dad to make this trip happen. The weather was so warm that we really did not need the blankets. You could lie on the floor and sweat without a blanket. I could sense that the two boys were not happy having to give up their bedroom to my Mom and Dad. I said nothing but I felt that if they were visiting us we would have to give up our bed to their mother and father. Exhaustion caught up with me and I slept.

Aunt Francis, with Moms help prepared lunch on Sunday morning.

In the meantime, Uncle Mike took us down into the basement to show us a project that he had been working on. His idea was to make recording discs out of glass discs. He was having trouble with the medium that he had to bake onto the glass that would hold the recording. Dad at this point let us know that Uncle Mike was a musician and that he was a member of the Pittsburgh Philharmonic Orchestra. Never mentioned what instrument he played.

A huge platter of pasta was the meal for our going away. It was good and of course very filling. Little did we know how much we would need that meal? We said our goodbyes and climbed into the Model A looking forward to an uneventful fairly quick trip home. Dad said that if everything went well we would be home in three or four hours. I think that the optimism that I have comes from my Father. Mom was the more practical one in our family.

We left Pittsburgh at noon. Mom's conversation with Dad centered on the visit.

"You know Vito, I have never met a person as stingy as your Aunt. How can she be that way to us when we are guests in her house? Especially when it is your nephew and his family that you have not seen for several years. If I didn't stand over her in the kitchen and made sure that she made enough sauce and cooked enough pasta, we would all four of us left there hungry"

"I don't know who my Aunt takes after but I agree she holds her purse tight with both hands!"

"When I went into the kitchen to check on the coffee, I couldn't believe it! After one hour the water was just beginning to change color. You saw it when we served it. It was just lightly colored water. If that was me, I would have been ashamed to serve it to my guests!"

They both laughed at the coffee episode and the dinner of the night before. Mom told Dad that she never met anyone like his Aunt Francis. She could squeeze a penny dry. Mom acknowledged that times were bad, but she said that his aunt was ridiculous. When you have guests, you try to do your best to accommodate them. You may pinch pennies with your immediate family but you do not pinch pennies when you have guests.

In route home, we had the same electrical problem that we suffered on the way to Pittsburgh. We lost four hours waiting at a service station. The mechanic had to go for a needed part. It was Sunday. Waiting at a service station is not very comfortable. There is nowhere to sit. There is no air conditioning. Dad was out talking to the service attendant.

We sat in the car with the windows down and complained about the heat. Johnny and I were sweating in the back seat. Mom was sweating in the front seat. We were complaining to Mom about the heat as if she could do anything about it. When we resumed our trip home, with the windows down and the wind blowing in our faces, we were cooled off and comfortable again.

At about six in the evening, we had a flat tire. We got out of the car and watched as Dad jacked up the car and removed the tire.

"Phil! Get the repair kit out from under the back seat!"

Without a word I climbed into the back of the car and lifted the seat to get the repair kit. I climbed out of the car. In the mean time Dad had loosened the tire from the rim and had pulled out the inner tube.

Dad inspected the inner tube.

"Here is the leak! Give me the kit! I need to use the scraper on the top."

I handed Dad the kit and he proceeded to scrape the area around the leak until it was good and clean.

"Hand me the glue! Take the cap off!"

Dad spread the glue liberally around the leak and handed the tube back.

"Put the cap back on! We don't know when we'll need it again. Now we have to wait for the glue to dry a little. Get me a patch. Not too big."

I reopened the kit and searched for what I thought was the right size patch.

After several minutes the glue was ready for the patch.

"Give me the patch Phil!"

Dad proceeded to place the patch on the inner tube. He then placed the inner tube on to the fender of the car and firmly rolled the round Tire Repair Kit over the patch.

"This is to make sure that the patch sticks well to the tube. We don't want to take a chance that the tube leaks when we put air in it."

After 10 minutes Dad put the inner tube back in to the tire and sealed the tire to the rim.

"Johnny! Get the air pump out of the back seat."

"I already have it ready for you Dad!"

"Oh! Good Johnny!"

Dad then pumped the air into the tire and placed the tire back on the axle. He tightened the lug nuts and lowered the car back on to the ground.

"OK! Put everything in the back seat! We're ready to go!"

By the time we were on the road again it was beginning to get dark. Dad turned the lights on. There were no lights. Dad cursed the mechanic in Italian.

"We have to look for another gas station," Dad said.

"Do you think we'll make it driving with no lights?" asked Mom.

"I'll just drive slow. I don't think the police are out this late".

"I hope you are right. I would not like to be stopped in the middle of the night!"

We'll be all right. I'll just take my time," said Dad.

Johnny and I just sat up straight. Watching the road in front of us to make sure that Dad didn't miss anything. So driving slowly, with no lights, we searched for a service station.

There were none open. It was Sunday and most closed at five in the afternoon since traffic was minimal. We were about twenty-five miles from home. We arrived home at twelve thirty, driving in the dark. Fortunately, very few people ventured out driving at night. We had not expected to be out this late either. We made it home. We were safe.

Mom said "Gratzia Dei!" Thank God.

"I am so glad that we are home! Lets go in and go to sleep in our own beds! C'mon Vito. Lets go.

"Thus was our trip to Pittsburgh. We did not make many trips in these days. Our farthest trips were to the lake that was about a 20-mile trip. I recall hearing about our local baker who had purchased a new Buick and drove all the way to Hot Springs Arkansas with only one flat tire. I think that this had to be some kind of record.

The Mason Woods

Chapter 11

The Mason Woods

The walk of five blocks to the edge of the woods is usually in haste. We relished every minute that we could spend among the trees. Once in the woods it is a two-minute walk to the giant oak tree with the cool spring flowing from beneath. The area surrounding the spring consists of three large hollows.

Hollows are crevasses or folds that were left in the earth during the ice age. The three hollows are parallel to each other. Two hundred feet separates each of them. Their lengths are identical. The height from top to bottom varies slightly. The only hollow with a small stream passing through it is the hollow with the spring.

At the end opposite the giant oak, about one mile away, is the railroad crossover. Each hollow is sealed with a huge man made dirt mound to make the railroad crossover. The mounds fill the hollows at their lowest point. The railroad track stands on the mound over one hundred feet above the lowest point in the hollows. A small four feet wide by four feet tall tunnel, constructed of cement block, is at the bottom of the hollow with the spring. This is the main hollow. The stream flows through the tunnel on its way to the river. The tunnel is two hundred feet long, and dark as night inside.

The main hollow is filled with magnificent tall silver birch, hickory, maple and oak on both slopes. Near the stream are the smaller vegetation such as ferns and wild flowers. There are a few green apple trees and wild hazelnut and blackberry bushes at the top of the slopes between the hollows. Sassafras, a root for making tea is in abundance.

The sassafras is harvested by pulling up the roots by the stem, and then washed in the spring water. Once home, the skin is removed in chips using a paring knife. You could use the chips immediately or air-dry the chips to provide tea for the winter. The chips are boiled in a pot of hot water and allowed to steep for several minutes. Then sweetened and enjoyed.

Many times we would harvest the sassafras and take it to the spring where we would wash it clean of any soil and then we would chew on it to extract the licorice flavor.

In July, the blackberries are everywhere. They provide nourishment as well as filling quarts to take home for mom's blackberry pies. Mom makes the most delicious blackberry pie ever. A slice of warm pie and a cold glass of milk was seventh heaven for Johnny and I.

The green apples are edible. They do not get very large however the fruit is very tasty. Some will be ready to be picked in August. These will provide a snack for the hungry young adventurers.

The hazelnuts will be ready to be picked in November. Since school will be in session at that time, the nuts would have to be harvested on a Saturday. Usually by the time we get there, the hazelnuts will be gone.

In the spring, the sweet intoxicating smell of the blossoming May Apple plant and the wild flowers that grow at the bottom of the hollows, lays heavy in the air. The oaks and birches seemingly cover and hold the warm moisture laden air and scents down in the hollow. The ferns and other small vegetation near the stream are as if in a greenhouse. Protected from the breezes and in great abundance.

Where the three hollows begin, lies an orchard of wild crab apple trees. The sweet, strong aroma during blossoming can be defected from afar. When the fruit appears on the branches, the crab apples, which are never more than a half-inch in diameter, are picked and launched on swift flights using a long slim branch from a young tree. The end of the branch is sharpened to a point. The point of the branch is pushed into the crab apple. Then with a whipping motion, the crab apple is sent on its way. The flexible slim branches make excellent crab apple launchers.

This is the time for crab apple wars. The friends that are in the Mason Woods choose sides then separate at a distance of approximately one hundred feet. Then begins the picking and launching of the crab apples. This activity continues until the novelty wears off. Or one group gives up. No one is usually hurt during these skirmishes. The potential for injury is there, however.

The main hollow, the one with the spring, is closest to our home on the East side of the city. The second hollow is not as beautiful to us as the other two hollows. There is no water passing through this hollow unless there is a heavy rain. Hollow number three, the deepest and least visited by us is the farthest away. One hundred-fifty feet deep at its farthest point from the crab apple orchard, at the railroad crossover, one mile away. Beyond hollow number three is the unknown.

The Mason Woods
Chapter 12
Adventure In The Woods

This day, there were only the three of us. When we arrived at the spring the first thing we did was to drink the cool spring water. The pool was about seven feet in diameter. You would kneel at the spring, below the huge oak. Drink with cupped hands or by touching your lips to the deceptively glassy plane of cool water. Deceptive in that this small spring kept a continual flow of rapidly moving water flowing thru the hollow. Then and only then were you ready for the day's adventures.

Down the slope to the stream to look for green frogs, called greenies. Or for crayfish, which we called crabs. Occasionally a pitch-black furry ground mole would be found digging swiftly into the ground as we approached. Within seconds it would disappear from sight. Moles are curious looking animals. Three to four inches long and an inch in diameter. Their front feet are disproportionately large and positioned towards the very front of their body to allow for swift digging. Almost as if attached to the head. They have a brilliant red nose that probably gets that way from burrowing into the ground.

Sometimes a squirrel would race through the weeds and go swiftly up a tree or a small rabbit would go scurrying towards the heavier brush.

Rocks in the stream are overturned trying to find the biggest crab. Smaller rocks are turned using a sturdy portion of branch found along the way. Larger rocks must be turned with your hands. When lifting a large rock on to its side, a swirl of silt would usually obscure the crayfish hiding under the rock for a short period until the flowing stream cleared the silt away and exposed the find. A splash in the water is usually a greenie leaping from the bank, seeking the protection of the stream. The adventurers continued slowly down the hollow, towards the railroad crossover. Small shallow pools in the stream provide more opportunities to search for frogs and crayfish.

"I've got one! I've got one!"

"What do you have?" Asked Johnny.

"The biggest crab you ever saw!"

"Let's see! Wow. Can I hold it?"

"Look! Its almost as big as my hand!"

"Let me hold it?" begged Johnny.

"Here! Take it! Don't drop it!"

"Wow! Where was it?"

"Under that big flat rock by the bush."

Boo and Johnny looked at the frightened creature. Daring each other to put their finger near the crab's pinchers.

"Here! Take it back!"

Boo took the crayfish and placed it into the stream.

"Lets see if there's bigger ones!"

They sloshed through the pool with tennis shoes and socks on. The stream created a pool that was six inches deep and ten feet wide. The water came from the spring and was cold and crystal clear.

"Where is Phil?" asked Boo.

"He's going down to the tunnel! We'll catch up later!"

The pair waded in the stream. Making their way towards the railroad crossover. Looking for anything that moved. Overturning rocks beneath the water. Sometimes a small crayfish would come scurrying out going towards deeper water.

"Look Boo! Here's a snake!"

"Where?"

"Here in front a me! It's alive! And it isn't moving!"

"Wait! I'll find a stick!

Boo returned with a slender tree branch and began prodding the snake with it. The snake tightened its coil. It was preparing to strike back. It then swiftly slithered into the taller grasses away from the stream.

"What was that?" asked Boo.

"A garden snake. They're harmless. We have to watch out for the copperheads. They're poisonous!"

Boo and Johnny continued slowly making their way down the stream and through the hollow.

Meanwhile, I arrived at the end of the first hollow at the bottom of the railroad crossover. Some one had cleared a group of small saplings that were growing near the stream. The saplings had been cut to almost ground level. Only small stumps about one to two inches above the ground and two inches in diameter remained. The area cleared was about five feet wide and fifteen feet in length. Someone must have had a purpose for making this clearing. The work to make the clearing would take at least a couple of days. I was puzzled.

I walked toward the tunnel that allowed the stream to pass under the railroad crossover. I could see that the heavy rain that we had last Friday had flooded the area in front of the tunnel. The normally tall grasses lay flat and were water logged. The pressure of the water caused this. You could see how deep the water was after the rain by looking at both sides of the hollow.

Bracing myself with one hand against the face of the tunnel, and keeping my feet out of the stream, I looked down through the 200-foot dark and narrow tunnel. I could see daylight at the other end. The tunnel was a very scary place. Then stepping in the stream. For young adventurers, with wild imaginations, this was really the height of adventure.

To walk through this small black hole, mossy walls closing in on you, feet sloshing in the water, rock hazards everywhere, not knowing what might be hiding in the water, the walk through seemed to last forever. Two hundred feet felt like a mile. And then, since there were no woods beyond the tunnel, you had the choice of returning through the tunnel or climbing the 100-foot embankment, crossing the railroad track and then going down the other slope to get back to the hollow. We usually chose the latter.

"Hey Phil!," yelled Johnny as he and Boo approached.

"What happened to the small trees that were here? They were all there last week!"

"I don't know. Looks like somebody cut them down. I can't figure it out!"

"Boo? Did you find any crabs?"

"Boy did I find a giant crab! It was big as my hand! Ask Johnny. He'll tell you."

"It was a big one," said Johnny.

"Do you guys want to wade through the tunnel? The water looks a little deeper today. The big rain we had Friday flooded the hollow"

The water passing through the tunnel is normally six to eight inches deep. Today it was over twelve inches deep in places. During a heavy rain, the water washing down from the sides of the hollow floods the tunnel completely, and creates a pond in front of the tunnel that is more than six feet deep and stretches upstream for eighty to one hundred feet. It submerges most all the vegetation at the bottom of the hollow. It would be very dangerous to wade into this swirling water. The pull of the water trying to get through the tunnel would pull you under and drown you.

"Yah! I can see where the water level was. It was pretty deep," said Johnny.

"I don't care! "I'm not going first this time!" said Boo. His voice had a slight sound of fear in it.

A few days ago when Boo was first to go into the tunnel and was half way through the tunnel something began splashing in the water in front of him. He bolted and struck his head slightly on the ceiling of the tunnel. He lost his balance on a slippery moss covered rock and fell into the shallow water. Fortunately, there were no rocks below him when he fell. He could have sustained a serious injury. Fortunately, the only injury was to his ego.

"OK. I'll go first, but you guys stay close behind me."

Boo and I responded.

"OK!"

Johnny stepped carefully into the stream. He stared towards the other end of the tunnel briefly, and then proceeded slowly and carefully forward into the tunnel.

"This water is ice cold!"

"Well, it's coming from the spring up there under the

old oak tree. It has to be cold."

Johnny realized that once you began, you would be called "chicken" if you backed out.

Inside the tunnel is a unique odor. The continuous flow of the fresh water coming from the spring mixed with the green velvety moss growing on the tunnel surface gives the air inside the tunnel a clean, cool, sweet smell. An odor that you can almost taste, a smell that once tasted, was lodged in the back of your memory forever. On warm days when there was no wind, the dampness and sweet odor inside the tunnel would become unbearable. Today was such a day.

The end of the tunnel looked like it was a mile away to Johnny. Boo stepped in behind Johnny and I took up the rear. Walking behind the leader made it almost impossible to see the end of the tunnel. This was not a place to be claustrophobic. To be afraid of being enclosed. It was as walking in total darkness.

"Careful! There's a big rock on the left side near the wall. Is it stuffy in here or is it me?"

No response.

"Hey! Are you guys there?"

"We're here! Just keep moving! It is stuffy in here. There's no wind blowing," I said.

We carefully made our way through the first part of the tunnel. Avoiding mossy rocks whenever possible. Johnny would always warn us of any obstacles coming up.

"So far, so good," said Johnny. "Why don't you guys

say something? Phil! Did you bring the knife with you?"

"Yah! I got it! Why? Do you want it?"

"Yah! Pass it up to me!"

"Here Boo. Pass it up."

Boo drops the knife.

"Oh heck! Wait let me see if I can find it."

Dragging his hand along the bottom, Boo feels the knife.

"Don't grab it by the blade! Just hand it to me when you fish it out of the water."

"Here!"

"Thanks. Are you O.K.?"

"I'm OK," said Boo.

"Let's get moving. It's too stuffy. Standing still in here makes it worse! Be careful with that knife!" I said.

We plodded on. Shoes sloshing. Carefully stepping over or around rocks. Sometimes losing our balance and tripping slightly. Inching towards the center of the tunnel.

The Mason Woods

Chapter 13

The Find

It seemed like hours, sloshing through the cold water before reaching the halfway point in the dark narrow tunnel. The low stone ceiling and close walls magnified the sound as we advanced. Walking hunched over. The air closed in making it difficult to breathe. No one talked. For Boo, and me it was even worse. We were behind Johnny. We could barely see beyond him to the daylight far ahead. The size of the tunnel, four feet wide and four feet high, made it impossible to walk side by side. For three boys, seven, eight, and nine, this was excitement. Not knowing what was up ahead. Testing our courage. Courage based on neither of us wanting to concede to fright. Tension that would be released when we exited the end of the darkness. Fear conquered. Relaxed.

Though we passed through this two hundred foot

long tunnel last week, it was still daunting to go through. Going through the tunnel was a ritual that took place at least three times during the grade school summer vacation.

Each time it was a test of courage. The water level earlier was about six inches deep. Most of the rocks washed in over the years protruded above the water. Now, because of the heavy rain we had last Friday, the depth of the water was about twelve inches. It flowed more rapidly. Most rocks normally above water were now hidden. You had to drag your feet along the bottom in order to detect them. Stepping or tripping on a hidden rock was hazardous. It was scary.

I looked back at the entrance. I could see the bright daylight framed by the dark black walls of the tunnel. The light reflecting on the surface of the stream.

"We're close to half way now! Let's just keep moving ahead!"

"Whoa! What's this! I stepped on something," said Johnny excitedly.

"There's something next to my foot that's squishy! Uh, Oh! It feels like a leg or something!"

"Come on! Quit trying to scare us! I'm sure Boo doesn't like it! I don't either."

Total silence. The three of us were buried in our own thoughts. Adrenaline skyrocketing. Running was upper most in my mind. Not a word was spoken for

120

what seemed like minutes. The only sound was the gurgling of the water splashing against the few protruding rocks as it raced through the tunnel on its way to the river.

"Boo! Feel down here were my foot is with your hand!"

"Not me! I am not going to touch no dead body! I'm scared! Let's get out of here!"

Johnny bent toward the flowing water. He moved his hand slowly over the object near his foot.

"I think it's a body! It feels like a leg!"

"Geese! Lets get out of here!"

We made an about face and ran toward the entrance as quick as the oncoming flowing water would let us. We covered the one hundred feet or so at record speed stumbling, slipping, tripping over rocks and falling into the water as we retreated.

"Hurry up Phil!" said Boo. "I want to get out of here!"

"Well stop pushing me! I'm going as fast as I can!"

We came out of the tunnel into the bright sunshine. I noticed a pale frightened look on Boos face. His baseball cap was pulled down tightly over his head making his ears bend forward. Gasping for air. Boo was the youngest. He tried to smile but a smile would not come. He swallowed the lump in his throat.

"Did anyone get hurt? Boo, are you OK?" Boo nodded a yes. His eyes were wide. Pants soaked.

"Did you hurt your knee," I asked as we stepped onto the bank.

Johnny seemed to be more composed. His eyeglasses were partially steamed. His blue jeans were also soaked. His left pant leg was ripped at the knee from falling on a rock as we rushed out of the tunnel.

"No, I'm OK."

"What was it, Johnny?"

"It was a persons leg! He must be dead or something! He's under water! I think he was laying on his back!"

"Could you tell who it was? It was probably too dark."

Muddy and wet we made our way up the steep one hundred foot slope. Our waterlogged sneakers were like ice skates on the slope. We could not grip the grass and dirt. Slipping and sliding, climbing using both hands and feet, we reached the top and the railroad tracks above the tunnel. We each let out a tired sigh of relief.

"Are you guys OK? " I asked.

"Yah! We're OK. Just tired from fighting that hill! Said Johnny.

"Yah! That was hard," said Boo.

"Boo! Are you all right? That didn't scare you did it?"

"Yah, I was scared! I am not ever going in that tunnel again! Nope! Not me! Never!"

"We have to go down to the police station and report it to Chief Ross!"

We started to walk towards town and the police station, a three-mile hike. We had the choice of walking along side the railroad track, or going home and getting our bikes.

"You know! It might be faster if we go home and get our bikes and ride down to the Police Station."

"You're right Johnny. It would be a lot faster. Let's go get them," I said.

We ran all the way home. Our water soaked sneakers and socks making odd sounds as we hurried along.

The Mason Woods

Chapter 14

Reporting The Find

We arrived home out of breath. A normal half-hour walk from the Mason Woods took us ten minutes running as fast as we could. Finding the body in the water pumped adrenaline into the three of us. We were excited to say the least.

"Let's meet at our house," said Johnny gasping for breath.

"OK," said Boo panting with his eyes rolling.

We wasted no time getting our bikes and riding as swiftly as we could to the police station. We took several shortcuts along the way.

When we arrived at the Police Station, our wet trousers were dry with mud caked all over them. Our shoes still sloshed and squeaked when we walked. We opened the door to the front office and walked towards the Desk Sergeant.

"May I help you boys?"

"Yah! We were out in the Mason Woods. We need to talk to Chief Ross!" I said nervously.

"What do you want to talk to him about?"

"Well, we were out in the woods going through one of the tunnels under the railroad and we think we found a dead body in the water!" said Johnny choking the words out of his mouth.

"A body! How do you know it was a body?"

"I felt the leg under the water!" said Johnny swallowing loudly.

The Desk Sergeant picked up his phone and rang the Chiefs office, which was located behind the Desk Sergeants front office. He told the Chief about the body.

Chief Ross came into the front office and looked at us. The Chief is a wiry man in his mid forties. He has red hair, blue eyes and a firm jaw. His lips never cracked a smile. His uniform fit him like a glove. His patent leather shoes glistened.

"Hi boys! I know you two," hesitating for a moment, looking us over from head to foot.

"Aren't you two Vito's sons? I used to work with your Dad back a few years ago in the mill. Fine Man."

What is your name he asked me?"

"My name is Phil and this is my brother John," I responded.

"And who are you young man?"

"This is Thomas's son. He lives down the street from us," said Johnny.

The Chief shook our hands and gave us a big smile. He took a seat on the bench located against the wall opposite the Sergeants desk.

"Come and have a seat. What's this about finding a body? Tell me about it."

Since Johnny was the only one who felt the leg, he proceeded to tell the Chief about what we were doing In the Mason Woods and how we found the body.

"Can you take me to where you found the body and show me?"

"Yes," said Johnny.

The chief turned to the Desk Sergeant.

"Anthony! I'm going to be gone for a while. I'm going to take a car and go over to the woods."

"Chief. From what they are saying, it's going to be a long walk and you may need some boots to go into the water."

"You're right. Thanks for reminding me. Get hold of the Coroner to meet us at the railroad crossing at Summit Street. Tell him to park there and then walk along the railroad track until he comes to the first hollow. We will meet him below at the tunnel entrance. Tell Charlie to bring some boots. He'll have the rest of the stuff that he needs," said Chief Ross.

"Boys! I want you to leave your bikes here. You can ride with me."

We were speechless as we looked at each others. Our eyes widened. Minds racing at the thought of riding in a police car. The police had just purchased three new 1941 Fords. One was the Chiefs car. The other two were patrol cars used by the police officers to patrol and do investigations. We were going to ride in the Chiefs car. Johnny got to ride in the front seat next to the Chief.

As we drove to the Mason Woods Chief Ross asked us what we were doing up in the woods. He wanted to know if we had our parent's permission to go there.

The drive lasted a quick ten minutes. We stepped out of the car. The Chief took his boots out of the trunk and carefully pulled them on over his shoes. He also took a flashlight.

"OK Boys! Lead me to where you went into the tunnel."

The four of us walked along the railroad track towards the top of the first hollow. The hollow was one quarter of a mile from the car. The three of us led the way. The steep one hundred foot slope was a bit difficult for the Chief to negotiate. His feet gave way several times on the way down. He grasped for shrubs to keep from sliding all the way down to the bottom. We were down at the bottom waiting for him, when he arrived.

"That's rough coming down that slope when you're old. You young guys go down the slope like mountain goats. It's way too fast for me. Stay here while I go in the tunnel. When Charlie shows up, tell him to wait out here for me."

"OK Chief!" said Johnny.

We waited impatiently to hear from the Chief. We stood in the water at the start of the tunnel watching the Chief making his way towards the middle of the tunnel. Flashlight beam glancing off the water and the sides of the tunnel. He arrived at where the body was.

"It's a body alright!" his voice echoed through the tunnel.

He then turned and came back to the opening. As the Chief was emerging from the tunnel, Charlie from the Coroners Office was slowly coming down the slope.

Charlie was somewhat rotund and a slip could cause him to come down the slope like a huge bowling ball.

"I heard you Chief catching his breath. Any idea who it might be?"

"He's under water. He looks familiar. We have to drag him out into the light. The water is shallow. About a foot deep. Did you bring some boots Charlie?"

"No I didn't. But that's all right. These are old shoes and pants."

"Well, Let's go ahead and drag him out. It's going to be a tight squeeze. Only one of us can fit in the space," said the Chief.

The two entered the tunnel. The Chief led the way. You could see that there was no way that Charlie was going to be much help pulling the body out. He could barely manage going into the tunnel.

We could hear the Chief and Charlie talking.

"This is quite a ways in!" said Charlie.

"About half way in. I don't know if the two of us can handle this!" said the Chief realizing that Charlie was not going to be much help.

"We may have to call Matt at the Fire Department and have his men come out here to remove the body. They have the equipment to do this sort of thing."

The Chief approached the location of the body then stepped past the body and flashed the light at the face beneath the water.

"Do you recognize him Charlie"

"I don't know for sure! Looks like it might be Squint!"

"You mean the Bookie?" asked Chief Ross.

"Yes! As far as I can tell looking at him under water."

"I don't believe that he was reported missing Charlie! If it is he this is a fresh crime of some sort. Let's get Matt to haul him out. Do we need to preserve the scene?"

"I don't think so chief. The flowing water has washed any evidence away. But that's up to you!"

"I'll go back to the car and radio Anthony and have him send Matt's boys out. I'll wait to hear from you about the details."

"OK Chief! I'll standby here until Matt's boys arrive."

"Thanks Charlie! Boys, are you ready to ride back with me?"

"Yah Chief!" said Johnny.

On the way back to the car, the Chief told us how the three of us have done an important service to the community. He did not know what happened here but it looked very suspicious. And he expressed his appreciation for a job well done.

The Chief drove to Boos house. Boos mother came to the door expecting bad news when she saw the Chief standing at her front door. She thought that maybe Boo was in trouble.

"Don't tell me that Thomas is in trouble?" she asked.

"No Mam! My name is Chief Ross!"

"I know who you are Chief!"

"Well Thomas and the two boys here have done a tremendous service to the City and I want you to know that he is safe with me and we are going to the Police Station. But you have nothing to worry about. OK?"

"OK Chief"

Chief Ross did not go into any details. He did say that Boo, Johnny and I were going to ride to the Police Station with him to pick up our bikes and we would be home soon. The same message was given to our Mother. Our Father and Boos Father were at work during the daytime.

Arriving in town, the Chief took us to the Isaly's ice cream parlor, next to the Robbins Theater and bought each of us a giant skyscraper cone of ice cream, and one for himself. He then drove us to the Police Station. We went to the Desk Sergeant.

"Anthony! We don't have a positive ID yet but it looked like it was Squint Fredrics body in the water. Charlie will call us with an id on the body. He did feel certain about who it was. I want you to make an entry on the blotter, about these young citizens doing their civic duty by reporting a crime to us. Enter each name. Also call Agnes at the Times and ask if she is interested in writing a story about these young men and how they helped the police.

In the meantime, I'll be in my office," said Chief Ross.

Thanks again Johnny! You too Phil. You too Boo," as he shook our hands. "Go straight home now because your parents are waiting for you."

We exited the police station, got on our bikes and drove home.

After supper that evening, Agnes from the Times Newspaper came to the house. Johnny went to Boos house to ask if Boo could come over to talk with Agnes. The three of us laid out all the details for Agnes to do her story. It took two hours.

The Mason Woods

Chapter 15

Back to the Woods

We did not have a full day to spend in the woods. We decided it would be best to ride our bikes and then walk them along the railroad tracks to the first hollow. We had much to discuss on the way. We felt strongly that Chief Ross would do a proper investigation and get the person who did Squint in. We hoped that information we gave him would lead back to the killer.

As we rode down the street towards the railroad tracks we decided to stop near the huge boulder that lay off the roadside. The boulder was made of sandstone and measured about ten feet in diameter. The effects of the wind and water over a long period of time had worn the surface until it was smooth. The boulder stood back about six feet from the edge of the street. Between the boulder and the street was a ditch that was eight feet deep that had been carved by running rainwater. It was always challenging and fun to leap from the edge of the road and onto the boulder.

"OK! Who's going first?"

"I'll go! Let me go first," stated Boo with a noticeable sound of excitement in his voice.

"I'm first!"

Being the youngest and shortest of the three, Boo had to go to the middle of the street and take a running start if he was to make it to the boulder. With his short legs moving as fast as they could, he ran towards the edge of the street and launched himself into the air and landed on the boulder.

Johnny and I cheered and acknowledged his achievement.

I went next then followed Johnny. There we stood on the boulder, conquerors! Getting down from the boulder was a simple walk onto the dirt that covered the other side and down the road a ways till you could easily get back onto the street.

We repeated the jumps until the novelty wore off, which was about ten minutes.

We then mounted our bikes and continued onward.

We arrived at the tunnel end of the first hollow. We left our bikes atop the slope near the railroad tracks. We began to move down the slope. Boo noticed a wire hanging from the tall elm tree that grew upwards from the middle of the slope. The elm tree towered over the hollow. One of its lower branches had a cable wrapped around it. Someone had climbed the tree, crawled out on the branch about twenty feet and wrapped the cable around the branch. Spikes were driven through the cable to secure it to the branch.

"Look! Someone made a swing! There's the loop at the end of the cable tied to the tree trunk," said Johnny.

The trio made their way to the tree. Someone had driven a spike into the trunk and fastened a clothesline from the swings loop to the tree.

The height from the branch to the floor of the hollow was at least seventy-five feet. The loop was a twelve-inch piece of lead pipe. The type that is used to transfer water in a house. The cable was passed through the pipe and the strands of the cable were opened and tied around the cable above the lead pipe. This made a perfect handle to hang onto for swinging down through the hollow. The arc of the swing would take you directly through the clearing where the young saplings had been cut down.

"So that's why those small saplings were cut. Remember when we came down through the bottom of the hollow the other day?"

"Yah! I remember!" said Boo.

"Lets try it out!" said Johnny excitedly.

"We can loosen the rope and climb back up the hill and pull the swing with us."

"OK! Lets take it up the hill and try it. I wonder who built this? You think it was the Baldwin St guys?"

"Yah. I think so. Those guys are the only ones crazy enough to climb the tree and go out on that limb. Loosen the rope Boo and lets go up the hill with It.," said Johnny.

As we went up the side of the slope holding the rope and pulling the swing handle up with us the handle came closer to us. We came to a point on the slope that seemed like the spot where you launch. You could reach the handle without using the rope.

"O.K. Guys. Since I am bigger than both of you, I'll test it out. If I make it, it'll be safe for you guys to swing," I said

"I'm not going on that thing," said Boo. "I don't want to get killed yet!"

"You don't have to if you don't want to."

"OK. Here goes!" I said excitedly.

I grasped the lead pipe and looked down toward the bottom of the hollow a long seventy-five feet below. I was scared and nervous. I launched from the slope. It was exhilarating

"Hang on tight Phil!" said Johnny.

The flight was taking me directly to where the saplings had been downed to almost ground level. As I was approaching the bottom of the arc, I heard and felt a crackling sound from the cable. My weight was beginning to stress the cable where it was tied above the lead pipe.

"Oh no! I hope it holds!" I yelled.

As the arc began to bottom out and my speed was at

its fastest the tie in the cable above the pipe came loose. The pipe slipped from the cable. My hands were still holding on to the pipe. I was airborne hurdling forward directly towards the sapling stumps sticking up out of the ground. I smashed into a stump with the full velocity of the pull of gravity. The outside of my left thigh took the blow. I lay there wondering if I was still alive.

Then I felt this sharp pain in my left thigh as I tried to move. I jumped up on my two feet. I tried to take a few steps forward. It was painful to move. Tears were welling up in my eyes. I felt like crying, but I held back. I did not want them to see me crying. Johnny and Boo were coming down the slope to help me. I felt my thigh carefully. It was not broken.

"Are you alright Phil? Geese did you fly through the air! When Boo and I saw that we thought you were a goner! Can you walk?"

"No! I can barely stand on it! My leg really hurts! I think you guys need to help get me up to my bike so I can go home!"

"OK. Boo get on his right side and I'll take the hurt side! We're just going to have to take our time to get up the hill. Let's see Phil, can you brace yourself on us and move forward?

"Try it!"

"Oh that hurts!"

"Try to keep the weight off your hurt leg. Lean on me and Boo! Keep your left foot off the ground. OK. Let's try to move forward. That's it. One step at a time."

The climb up the hill took fifteen minutes. My thigh was really hurting now.

"Can you get up on the bike? Stand on the right side and swing your bad leg over!"

I limped to the right side of the bike. I couldn't lift my left leg over the bike.

"I have to get on the left side and see if I can stand on my left leg and throw my right leg over!"

I moved around to the left side of the bike. I tried to throw my right leg over the bike but when I lifted, the pain in my left leg became unbearable.

"Just a minute! Boo and me will tilt the bike towards the left and you should make it then! Grab the frame on the right side Boo and tilt it left with me."

That's right! Get your leg over Phil! Yah! That's it! Easy! Easy! OK.

"Boo! Lets straighten it up."

I was on the bike. Now what? I could not move my leg to work the pedals.

"Guys! I cannot work the pedals! One of you is going to push me home!"

"Johnny! Let Boo handle the other bikes and you push me!"

"O.K.! Boo can you handle the bikes?"

"Yah! I can get them home!"

So my brother and Boo were able to get me home.

"Johnny! Whatever you do don't say anything to Mom. Promise me!"

"I won't! But you know Mom! She'll wonder why we're home so early and she'll come to see if something is wrong!"

And as was usually the case when I got hurt, I went into the house by the side door. Limping, I went directly to my bedroom and flopped on my bed. Mom heard me coming in. Of course, since I have done this same thing so many times before, sneaking in injured from doing some foolish thing, Mom knew immediately that something wasn't right. She waited ten minutes to see if I would come out of the bedroom. When I didn't come out, she came into the bedroom.

"What happened to you this time Phillip?"

"I cannot fool you Mom. I knew you would be in here," I said, lying on the bed.

"I'm O.K. I just fell and hurt my leg."

Trying not to worry her.

"I'll be alright. I just need to rest a while."

"You didn't sprain an ankle again, did you?"

"No Mom. I didn't. I'll be OK!"

I didn't leave the bedroom until Dad came home from work, and it was time for supper. I limped from the bedroom making sure that no one was in the kitchen or at the dining table as I came in. I took my seat and sat there through supper. Afterwards while no one was looking, I sneaked back into the bedroom. Only my brother knew what had happened and he wasn't saying anything.

The next morning I was very sore but I could walk better. I did not go back to the Mason Woods for several days. The weather was cloudy with some rain. There was little fun to be had in the woods when it was wet.

I stayed around the house building a model airplane in the small room in the basement. Cutting out the planes pieces from the balsa wood that they were stamped on with one of my fathers' double-edged razor blades required a steady hand and much patience. One slight slip meant that you had to take a piece of balsa wood and try to trace the pattern as accurately as you could and then try once again to cut it out

Model Planes were very inexpensive at this time. You could buy a kit for five cents. For twenty-five cents you could buy some large models. Putting the plane together after the parts were cut out was also a challenge. The glue used to assemble the plane made you lightheaded. I had to keep the basement window ajar to let the fumes out.

The Mason Woods
Chapter 16

The Heroes

Two days after we reported the find of the body to the Chief the local newspaper headline read "Young Locals Help Police". Beneath were all the details of how Johnny, Boo and I had found the body of Squint Fredrics, a well-known local shady character, sometimes called the "Bookmaker", under water in a stream in Mason Woods. It went on to give details about Squint and his family. In the write up it mentioned that Squint had told his wife that he was going to Detroit for one week. He was picked up on Friday morning in the rain by a man who appeared to be known to Squint. She did not remember his name but the license plate on the car was a Michigan plate.

Squint is well known through out the area, from Cleveland to Pittsburgh. Everyone knows the business that he runs. He has a small frame building on a corner on the East side of town. From this building, he runs his book making business. Basically, a bookmaker takes bets on various activities. The most popular betting involved the publishing of certain financial data daily by the Treasury Department of the United States. Ironic that they would use Treasury data since gambling is illegal. The bet is to guess the last three numbers of that certain data. If you guess the numbers in the order that they are published, you receive five hundred times the amount you bet. You could also box the numbers, which means that your numbers could be in any order. For this you receive two hundred fifty times your bet. Squint has bookies that canvass the entire city every day.

I remember Grandma betting two cents on two different sets of numbers. When someone won, the news got around fast and more people would join the betting. The bookies made certain of that. The bookie that canvassed our neighborhood was named Joe. Joe had a family of five and had no other means of earning money that anyone knew of. The bookmaking business must pay well.

Squint was tied in with the mob. His boss was a man in one of the larger nearby cities. The mob front in the nearby city was a bar on the shady side of town known to the locals as thirty-seven and a half. The bar had the same name. A friend's father, whose name is Carl, was looking for work. Carl had been unemployed for some time and had two small children and a wife to feed. Not knowing what kind of place this bar was, he ventured into the bar and asked for a job. He was told he could start the next day.

Mid afternoon of the next day, the owner, a member of the mob, received a phone call. He hurriedly went to Carl who was behind the bar and told him that no matter what happened, he was to tell who ever came into the bar, that he was the owner. The owner left the bar almost running. Ten minutes later, several investigators from the U.S. Treasury Department came into the bar and asked for the owner. Carl said that he was the owner. He spent one year in the county jail.

A city favorite for placing bets was the East Side Barber Shop. The barber shop is really a house on a corner. The front room had been made into a barber shop. The barber and his family lived in the back rooms and upstairs. As a child, to watch the people entering and exiting, school teachers, politicians, the Chief of Police, made you wonder what was going on in there besides cutting hair. The majority who entered the small one-man barbershop were in there for no more than five minutes. Enough time for the barber to stop cutting hair and write down the numbers and collect the money to place a bet.

One day, about a year ago, the local newspaper had an article announcing that two U.S. Treasury Department Agents were coming into town to investigate the possibility of gambling and crime going on in our small city. Several days later the newspaper gave an account of the agents meeting with Chief Ross and the mayor. The newspaper reported that the Feds found no gambling or criminal activity going on in the city. While this so called investigation was going on, book making and whatever else did not take a holiday. It continued while the investigation was being performed.

Johnny, Boo and I decided to snoop around the neighborhood to find out what had happened to Squint. The best place to get any information is the barbershop. If anybody knows anything, it will be talked about in the East Side Barber Shop.

This time of year, mid June, the barbershop windows are kept open. You could sit under a window and hear everything that was talked about inside and go unnoticed. I took a pack of playing cards from the kitchen drawer and brought it with us.

It is nine o'clock. Opening time for the barbershop. We went to the window that was hidden from the street. Here we would go unnoticed. If someone did see us, we were just three kids playing cards. The pair of scraggly shrubs made it difficult for passersby to see us.

We were there for all of fifteen minutes when two men entered the barber shop. The talk was about Squint.

"Hey barber, how you doing?"

"Hey! How are things in Sharon?" asked the barber.

"Everything is OK now that we got rid of the problem!"

144

"Are you talking about Squint?"

"Who else! That guy was giving us a lot of problems. A lot of problems." said the first voice.

"Da boss put out the contract last week! We're surprised that they found him so quick!" said the second voice.

"Is da business still OK? I mean are the collections still coming in?"

I asked Boo to go around the back of the building and check the License plate numbers on the car while they were inside the barbershop.

"No! Nobody has been around. I haven't seen Joe. He usually comes in and collects every afternoon! But he hasn't come by. No one has even come by asking to get some action!" said the barber.

"Well, the boss has setup a new guy and he will be contacting everyone so that everything can continue like before! I think he is going to use Squints Place to operate from, temporarily."

Boo returned.

"Who did the hit?" asked the barber.

"Some guy that goes by the name Feets. He's outa Detroit.," said the first voice.

"Isn't he the one who ran the Jungle Inn?"

"Yah. That's him.," said the second voice. "I phoned him yesterday when the newspaper came out. He took Squint out there near the railroad tracks and shot him and pushed him down a hill and he tumbled into a pond at the bottom."

"Well, Joe will let me know when he wants me to start up. I'll wait for his go ahead."

"OK. barber! You take care a yourself and keep your nose clean! See Yah!"

The three of us slipped from below the window and went out to the sidewalk to get a better look as they came out of the barbershop, onto the front porch. They stood for a few seconds as if contemplating their next move. They then came down the seven steps to the sidewalk and went around the corner to their car. Not a word was spoken. They drove off. We made a good mental note of their features. Boo had written the numbers of the Pennsylvania license plate on their car, in the sand.

"Good job Boo! Great thinking!"

"Let's go next door to Aunt Grace and see if we can borrow a piece of paper to write the license number down." I said.

After that was taken care of, we went to Boos house and sat on the front porch.

"What are we going to do now?" Asked Johnny. "We can't go to Chief Ross."

"Why not? Just because he might bet the numbers, doesn't mean that he is on the side of the mob. I think we should go downtown and tell him right away."

What do you think Boo?"

Boo shrugged his shoulders, signifying that he would go along with whatever we wanted to do.

146

"I think we have to tell somebody, and Chief Ross is the right guy!"

"OK! Lets get on our bikes and go down to the police station," said Johnny.

The two-mile ride took fifteen minutes. We arrived and parked our bikes. We went into the station. Anthony was on the desk.

"Hi fellahs! What's new today?"

"We need to talk with the Chief," I said.

"Chief's not here right now. He went to a meeting at the municipal building. He should be back here in a few minutes. Do you want to wait for him?"

"No. We'll be back in a little bit. We're going to go over to Isaly's to get a cone."

"OK! I'll tell the Chief you fellahs came in. See you in a little while."

We rode our bikes to the ice cream parlor two blocks away. We had ten cents between us. The ice cream parlor owner Mr. Ritchie recognized us from our pictures in the local newspaper and gave each of us a free skyscraper cone. We sat in the cool parlor, enjoying the free cones. Mr. Ritchie came over introduced himself and sat with us.

"Where do you boys live?"

"On the East side," Said Johnny.

"That was a great thing that you did! I am glad that there are children around that have respect for people, and for the law. You tell your mothers and fathers that the city is very proud of you three boys. I have a son, John, who is in the Marines. He is in

Hawaii. He likes it over there. He writes home and tells me and his mother that he would like to live there when he gets out."

"If he stays there, will you move out there too Mr. Ritchie?" I asked.

"Maybe we will. It all depends on how his mother feels about it. Maybe we can sell ice cream in Hawaii."

He got up and went behind the counter to wait on a customer that had entered.

A few minutes later the Chief walks in. He greets Mr. Ritchie.

"Hi John! How you doing? Hear anything from Junior?

"Yah Chief! Received a letter from him yesterday. He's doing fine! Thanks for asking!"

The chief walks to our table with a smile playing on his face.

"Hi fellahs!" coming towards our table and sitting down. "What do you three have for me this morning?"

"Chief! We found something out that we need to tell you about."

"Is it about Squint?" he asked.

"Yes," I said.

"Well, finish up your cones and lets go back to the office to talk."

148

The Chief had walked over to the ice cream parlor from the police station. So we walked back with him pushing our bikes along.

Inside the office, we proceeded to tell the Chief about what we had seen and heard at the barbershop.

"Chief! The three of us were sitting outside the side window at the barbershop playing cards when two guys came in and talked to the Barber. The barber asked them if they knew about Squint? One of the guys told the barber that they knew the guy who killed him. His name is Feets and he's from Detroit."

"This is good information! You three are turning out to be darn good detectives! If you were older I would give each of you a job in the police department."

"Boo also got their license plate number!"

We gave him the license plate number.

"Thank you very much boys! Do not tell anyone what you just told me! There is an investigation going on!"

Our police station is not very big. The Chief has seven patrolmen who alternate as desk sergeants. The midnight shift only has the desk sergeant. No patrolmen. During the day Monday through Friday from 8:00 Am till 5:00 PM, the Chief is there with a desk sergeant and a patrolman. In the Afternoon it is a desk sergeant and a patrolman. On weekends it is an as required situation. Someone is always on call for emergencies. The Chief does all investigations. We cannot afford detectives in our small town.

When we arrived home, we realized that we still had much of the day left. We decided to go spend some time in the woods.

The Mason Woods
Chapter 17
The Swing

The next day, Tuesday, we went back to the woods. After our half hour walk from home, a drink of the cool spring water felt good. Just to stand near the spring in the cool shade of the huge oak tree gave you a sense of anticipation. The tree filled hollow was quiet and peaceful. The only sounds were those of the birds and the gurgling of the stream flowing down the slope towards the bottom of the hollow.

"Where are we going?"

"Where do you want to go Boo?"

"Let's go down and check out the swing!"

"What do you think Phil?"

"Yah! Sounds good to me! But don't think that I'm going on that thing again! I had enough."

"OK, Let's go down to the swing!" said Johnny.

We proceeded down the slope leading from the

spring to the bottom of the hollow. You could hear birds chirping in the trees. Occasionally a bird would fly close above our heads. Before long, as we walked along the stream, keeping our eyes out for large crabs, several small birds began to screech as they flew at our heads. They were attacking us. We began to run. We finally outran the birds.

"You know what that was about? They're nesting! They are protecting their eggs or small birds!" I explained.

"I never heard of that! Is that true or are you making it up?"

"It's true, Boo! That's what they do. They never crash into you though. But that's what they do," responded Johnny.

The rest of the walk toward the end of the hollow was uneventful. No large crabs to see. Small ones either. As we approached the tunnel, we heard voices. Laughing and talking. The forest muffled the sounds. As we advanced and the railroad slope became visible, we could see that there were several boys up on the side of the slope where the swing was located. We recognized them. They were not from our neighborhood. They lived on a street that was closer to the Mason Woods.

"Hey Stash! What are you guys up too? Hi George. Hi Yow!" I yelled from the bottom of the hollow.

Stash and George are brothers. They are the same age. Not twins but born eleven months apart. They live on Baldwin Street. Baldwin is two blocks closer to Mason Woods than our street. They are sons of

152

immigrants that came from Serbia. They are the youngest of five brothers. I go to school with Stash and George. Stash is more social and friendlier then George. Stash liked to be involved. George on the other hand was happiest when left alone. The difference between them is clearly visible as they stand side by side. No words spoken. The three of us are in the same class in school.

In History class two years ago, in the third grade, the teacher was calling on each of us to read one paragraph out of the History textbook. When George was called on to read, he had a difficult word to read that George had never seen before. The word was Egypt. George nonchalantly read the sentence and pronounced the word as Egg-wiped. Phonetically, he was correct. However the entire class and the teacher broke out in laughter. The teacher caught herself immediately and apologized to George, told him how to pronounce the word and then asked him to read the paragraph again from the beginning.

Yow was nine years old and his parents came from Poland. Two years earlier, while playing in the field with several guys from Baldwin Street, he was accidentally shot in the left eye with an arrow. He got his name Yow from the scream when the arrow punctured his eye.

"Hi Phil!" Stash was standing above on the slope with his hands grasping the swing.

"We built this swing last week. It's a lot of fun! Come up and try it!"

"I already tried it! Last week! It broke and I hurt my leg on one of these stumps down here!"

"Are you OK?”

"Yes! It took a day or two but I'm alright now!" as we arrived at the swing.

"Here! Watch! I'll show you how this works!"

Stash leaped from the slope holding both hands on the cross bar. He came down the slope legs raised and swung over the stump area and up in the air over the bottom of the hollow. He was at least fifty feet in the air. He then returned over the stumps and up the slope back to where he started.

"How did you like that Phil?"

"That was really great! I don't know! How did you fix the pipe?"

"We put a clamp on the cable above the pipe so that it won't come loose. Do you want to try it?"

"I don't know Stash! I'm a little heavier than you."

"My brother Goochi tested it after we put the clamp on and it held him. He's bigger than any of us. Here! You want to try it?" said Stash.

This was a challenge. If I didn't try it, I would fall into the ranks of the sissies.

"Go head and try it Phil!" said Johnny. "It should hold you now!"

"Well. OK. But remember, if something happens, we don't have our bikes here. That means that you or Boo have to go home and get my bike!"

"Nothings going to happen! You want me or Boo to go first?"

"You won't catch me on that thing! No way!" said Boo.

"No. I'll try it! Hand me the rope Stash!"

The swing was all that I expected it to be and more. Looking down, the height at the end of the arc was higher above the ground than I thought it would be. It was a great ride.

"Wow! That's really something!" I said as my feet landed on the slope.

"Who went up on to the branch to tie the cable?"

"My brother Goochi did that for us, He had to drive spikes into the side of the tree to get up there. Then he worked his way out on the branch and nailed the cable in place."

"Your brother is crazy! That branch is one hundred twenty-five feet above the bottom of the hollow! That branch goes out away from the trunk about forty feet! Man, I would never do that. For nobody!"

We all spent an hour or so having fun with the swing. Boo reluctantly gave it a try. I don't think he enjoyed it as much as the rest of us. He did not go on it again. Boo was the youngest in the gang and no one blamed him for not going on the swing again. We did tell him that we were all proud of him.

"Phil! Want to see what I found earlier?

"Yah George! What did you find?"

"Come over here were I have my sweater." We walked to his sweater.

"Here! Look at this!" said George as he unwrapped his sweater showing a pistol.

"Where did you find it?"

"It was over there near the railroad tracks, in the tall grass. Someone must have lost it!"

"Show me where it was?"

We walked about 50 yards from the swing to a patch of high grass.

"It was right in here!"

"It wasn't covered up or anything?"

"No!" said George.

"Did you hear about the body we found in the tunnel?"

"No! Who was it?"

"It was Squint! The bookie."

"When did it happen?"

"We found him last week! He was under water half way into the tunnel with his face up! The killer must have shot him up here and he fell down the slope into the water! Remember! It rained last week on Friday! The hollow must have flooded and washed the body into the tunnel. You know George, you should probably take that gun down to the police station!"

"Why should I do that? I found it, so it's mine!"

"Yah, but that gun was used to kill Squint! It could help. the police catch the shooter!"

"Well, then you take it down there! I'm not going there for anyone!"

"But you found it! I didn't. I'll go with you if you

want me too! But you found it!""No!" said George.

"I won't go down there! Here! You take it!"

"George! The police searched the area looking for anything that could help them and you found the gun. They didn't find it! You did! Can I at least tell the Chief that you found it?" asked Phil

"No! I don't want any part of it just give it to them!"

"OK! I'll do it!"

We walked back to the swing.

"Hey Johnny! I'm going back down to see Chief Ross! Do you want to go with me?"

"I'll go with you! Maybe well get another free ice cream cone!"said Boo.

"Yah! Let's go!" said Johnny.

We said our goodbyes to the Baldwin Street guys and proceeded towards home.

"What are we going to tell the Chief?" asked Boo.

"We have to tell him that we found it in the high grass near the railroad."

"Will he believe you?" asked Johnny.

"I think so. We just won't tell him anything more."

We arrived home got our bikes and rode to town.

The Mason Woods
Chapter 18

Information Central

On Sunday we went with the neighborhood gang to the Warner Theater for our usual entertainment. We returned home with the same discussions about the conclusion of the weekly serial and the doom of the hero.

That night, Sunday night around midnight there was a loud explosion that awakened me. It was not too far from our house. It was so strong that the windowpanes rattled in their frames. I lay there and wondered what had happened. Johnny and I shared the same bed. The boom did not disturb him. I fell back to asleep.

The next morning when we got to the breakfast table Mom asked if we heard the noise.

"Yes Mom! I heard it! What was it? Do you know?"

"Your father went out to see what happened when

we heard the loud noise. Some of the other men were outside when Dad came out. They heard the fire trucks a couple of blocks away. They found out that someone blew up Squint Fredrics building!"

"The bookie Joint?"

"Yes. The bookie joint." said Mom. "So you kids better watch out. There's a lot of trouble around here."

"We're always careful Mom!" said Johnny.

We waited for Boo to come over. We decided that we should go sit under the window at the barbershop again. I had the deck of cards in my pocket. It was early Monday morning. The barber shop had opened about ten minutes ago. There were no customers yet. Time dragged on. We played Go Fish. At about eleven o'clock we heard a car pull up on the other side of the building. Two doors slammed shut so we knew that at least two people came out of the car.

A voice yelled.

"City police! Hands up high over your heads! Do it NOW!"

We edged towards the side of the building to peek at what was going on. There was Chief Ross and another policeman pointing their guns. We could not see who they were pointed at. So we went around to the backside of the barbershop and peeked. We saw the two men who had come to the barber shop last week to talk to the barber about Squints murder. They were standing there with their hands up high.

"Turn around!" yelled the policeman as he and the

Chief approached the two.

The Chief and the policeman each took one man and put handcuffs on them. They then led them to the police car that was parked in a driveway, hidden by a row of shrubs. They then left for the police station.

"Boy! That was something, to see Chief Ross in action! Those cops are tough!"

"Yah!" said Boo. "They're tough! Do you guys think that we need to go down to the police station?"

"No. If the Chief needs us he'll come and get us. I think he saw the Pennsylvania license plates. That's how he knew who they were." I said.

"Are you guys ready to go?" asked Boo.

"No! We're not done here yet. We want to see if anyone comes here and talks about blowing up Squints Joint last night."

"Right!" said Johnny.

At one-thirty, a customer comes into the barber shop.

"Hi barber! Are you cutting any hair today?"

"No. Parrot. Mondays are always my slow day. Have a seat. Did you hear about Squints?"

"Who didn't? That boom knocked me out of bed. You know who was behind that don't you?"

"No! I'm like you! It woke me up. I got up and heard the fire trucks so I headed toward the sound and saw that Squints joint was in flames."

"Well, don't tell anyone, but it was Mugsy. You know who I mean. He got twenty-five grand for doing the job."

"Who hired him? asked the barber.

"That gang out of Detroit! I think they're called the Purple Gang or something like that. I think that they're trying to muscle out the Sharon people."

The conversation in the barber shop turned to sports. The barber finished Parrots haircut and Parrot left. We heard the barber dialing his telephone.

"Hi! I need to talk to the Chief"

A brief pause waiting for the Chief to answer.

"Hello Chief! This is Willy. I got some news for you on the Joint."

Pause for the Chief to respond.

"Oh! OK! I heard the same thing! Talk to you later."

The barber hung up.

It felt good to find out that the barber was working with the Chief. The barber shop was the central point for finding out all the goings on in the community as well as national and global issues. People constantly come in to find out what was going on in the community. They would also add their bit of knowledge to whatever the conversation. It was a forum for exchanging information on any subject. The barber was the beneficiary of all the knowledge. He was a sharp individual and could screen out all the misinformation after hearing virtually all sides of an issue.

He was also working both sides by booking numbers

for the mob and keeping in close touch with Chief Ross. This was something that had to be kept quiet. It could put the barber in harms way if we talked to anyone about it. We decided that it would be best for us to forget about this discovery and not mention what we knew to anyone including the barber and Chief Ross.

We went home satisfied that the Chief had things under control. The Treasury Agents coming to town to check on crime and gambling as reported in the newspaper may have been to give the Mob a false sense of security about what they were doing.

The Mason Woods

Chapter 19

Sorting It Out

Feets the alleged killer of Squint Fredrics was transferred from a jail in Detroit to the county jail in our area to be tried for murder. They could find no connection between him and the notorious Purple Gang, which was well known in the Detroit area. He was transferred from Detroit using the railways, escorted by a County Sheriffs Deputy and as reported by the local newspaper, it went as planned. The trial was scheduled to start on the coming Monday.

The reporting in the local newspaper angered the people of our small city. The newspaper called it a trial to satisfy the hoodlums and Squint and Feets were both involved with the mob and the courts were being used to appease the other gang members.

165

The topic of conversation at the barbershop was the up coming trial and what was being reported in the newspaper. However, it is still the duty of the courts to bring justice to this act of murder according to what we overheard from the barber. Willy the barber was usually right.

The barber was in a position to hear all sides of an argument from his customers. He was armed with all the right answers to anyone who made statements that were not in line with the majority of the thinking on the subject. The customers knew that the barber had heard all sides and was intelligent enough to arrive at an educated opinion that most respected. Once in a while there would be one person who did not agree with his opinion and this usually resulted in a wager being made. The barber usually won these.

The dynamiting of Squints building was still under investigation. Given the capabilities of the time, the only way the perpetrator would be found is by questioning people in the neighborhood, or someone coming forward and pointing the finger, then that person was given the protection of anonymity by the police for his assistance. The police would then use whatever means at their disposal to obtain a confession from the suspect. This method was far from fool proof.

There were innocent people who could not provide acceptable alibis and spent jail time as the consequence. An example of this is a young man from our neighborhood, nineteen years old, who was charged with a crime that he did not commit. He swore that he had nothing to do with the robbery and wasn't even near the place when it occurred. He was found guilty and sentenced to twenty-five years in the State penitentiary. He hung himself in his jail cell one year later. I am sure that this was not unique to our city.

Grandma sat on the front porch enjoying the company of her three daughters and the warmth of the summer sunshine. She sighted Joe the Bookie who had worked for Squint Fredrics walking down the sidewalk. The sidewalk was no more than thirty feet from the front porch.

"Joe, come over here I want to talk to you," called Grandma.

"Ciao signora! Greeted Joe. What a beautiful day."

"Joe, are you picking up the numbers for today? I have three sets of numbers I would like to give you," stated Grandma.

"Signora, I am not collecting numbers today."

"And why not," she asked.

"The business is shut down for a little while, but it should be starting up very soon! If it doesn't start up soon, I will have to go out and find a job."

"Arrivederci signora," as Joe walked off on down the street."

Grandma snickered.

"Joe is going to have a tough time now. He has had it easy for many years. What kind of job can he get at his age? He is almost sixty years old and very heavy. His walk is very labored and his arms swing back and forth in an arc away from his sides, front to back."

"I feel sorry for Joe. He is a good man with a nice large family." said Mom

The sisters agreed.

Joe the Bookie lived across the street and three houses away from us. His was the newest house on the street. It was also the largest. He had it built three years ago. His family of seven kept to themselves. Actually, no one ever saw them. Mom knew his wife but had not spoken to her for many years.

Joe the Bookie had been served a subpoena to appear in court as a witness because of his known association with Squint Fredrics. Everyone including Chief Ross knew what Joe did.

They knew what Squint did. Even though gambling was illegal at this time, law enforcement did not have the available manpower or the desire to enforce the Federal Governments Gambling Laws. I guess the universal feeling of the time was to let the U.S. Government handle situations concerned with gambling. Of course this trial was not about gambling. It was about murder. Joe would be handled as if he were an employee of Squint Fredrics business. The gambling part would more than likely never be addressed.

The Mason Woods

Chapter 20

It All Comes Together

Anthony sat at the front desk. Anthony was a huge muscular guy. You could tell that he worked out frequently. He stood six feet four inches and weighed well over two hundred pounds. The starched grey shirt he wore with the officers badge pinned on the left pocket, a silver chained whistle attached to his right pocket and the perfectly tied dark blue tie made him look every bit the part of Desk Sergeant. His presence behind the desk made the desk look small. He had an olive complexion. His face was solid, stern and clean-shaven. He had a dark head of hair parted on the left side and dark eyes peering out from beneath his heavy dark eyebrows. Anthony looked the type that you did not want to say any wrong things too. Anthony lived on our side of town, a few blocks from where we lived. Occasionally we would play baseball with his younger stepbrother, Jimmy.

"Hi! Are you here to see the Chief?"

"Yes we are."

"Let me see if he's busy!"

Anthony telephoned the chief in the back office.

"Go in fellahs!" said Anthony.

We entered the Chiefs office. It was a small room with a desk like a schoolteacher has in the classroom. On the desk was a telephone and an in-basket loaded with papers. On the wall was a certificate from the Police Academy of the State of Ohio, and a commendation certificate from the Governor of the State. The Chief sat behind the desk.

"Hi fellahs! What's going on today? Find anymore bodies?" A smile came across his face.

"Chief! We were over at the tunnel and we found this pistol in the high grass near the railroad tracks. We thought that it might be important.," said Johnny.

"You bet!" said the Chief as he got up and came over to us and took the pistol.

"That pistol is an important piece of evidence. It was used to shoot Squint Fredrics! Thank you very much!"

The Chief shook hands with each of us.

"The police in Detroit have Feets in jail! This gun will help put him in jail for a long long time!"

The Chief went out to the Desk Sergeant. We followed him.

"Anthony! Get an evidence envelope and put this pistol in it. Mark it as evidence for the Squint Fredrics case."

"OK Chief!"

"How would you fellahs like an ice cream cone?" said the Chief reaching into his pocket and pulling out a few coins.

"Here! One nickel for you Phil, one for you Johnny and last but not least, one for you Thomas! You have a nickname don't you?"

"Yes sir! They call me Boo!"

"Who gave you that name?"

"My older brother Ralph did!"

"Well! It is different. OK fellahs! Thanks once again for your help!"

We mounted our bikes and went directly to the ice cream parlor.

"Hi Mr. Ritchie!" I said as we entered.

We each plunked down our nickels.

"Hi fellahs! What can I get for you?" Taking the ice cream scoop in his hand.

"I would like a chocolate skyscraper please!"

"I'll have the same!" said Johnny.

171

"Me too!" said Boo.

Mr. Ritchie was very generous with the ice cream on our skyscraper cones.

"Thanks for your business!"

We sat at a table in the corner of the room discussing what we were going to do for the rest of the day.

"Why don't we take a ride out to the pool? We can see who's out there!" I said.

"No. I don't want to go." said Johnny.

"Let's just go home for the rest of the day. We can play some cards on the front porch."

"OK! But if we sit around the house Mom will think that there is something wrong. Sick or something!"

"Let's go over to my house and play cards on the front porch! We have a card table and chairs that we can use!" said Boo.

We played a game called War. Boos Mom brought out some fresh made lemonade for us. She asked what we were doing home already. It was only two o'clock. We explained what we had done and that we went down to give the pistol to Chief Ross.

Johnny and I got home at four o'clock. We cleaned up in anticipation that Dad would soon be home.

Dad brought home a piece of candy for us in his lunch bucket once in a great while.

Today he had candy for us. His instructions as always were not to eat the candy until we had supper. Dad went to clean up and change for supper.

The suppers during the week were not my favorite meals. Although Johnny liked the food, I was always the one who needed to be encouraged by Dad. Threatened is probably the right word. Dad never laid a hand on either of us. With his certain look and his firm voice, you did what he wanted you to do. But he knew deep down that I did not like the peasant style of cooking that they were accustomed to in Puglia. Mom understood but never stepped in. She never undermined Dad in cases involving the two of us. When she saw that I was down in the dumps, she would give me a dime. I would go to the grocery store on the corner and buy a pound of bologna and a loaf of bread. I would bring them home and make bologna sandwiches slathered with a ton of mustard. I would eat until I could not take another bite. My down in the dumps was quickly gone.

The Mason Woods
Chapter 21

The Results

At Nine O'clock on Monday morning, the trial began. The local newspaper reported on Tuesday that the proceedings started out slow. The Honorable Judge Griffin presided. Both the prosecutor Mr. Gronert and the defense council Frank Mastol were very careful during the presentation of their opening statements. The newspaper reported that the prosecutor was making sure that all the details of the offense were being covered and that the alleged murderer would be sentenced properly. The prosecutor's case was strong. He had the weapon used to kill Squint Fredrics, and prints on the weapon matched Feets fingerprints. He also had the two mobster witnesses from Detroit who knew that Feets was the killer. The newspaper said that His full name was Albert Williams. Feets was his gangland name.

The newspaper account of the trial said that the prosecutions star witness was Joe Salandra. Joe the bookie. Joe took the stand on Monday afternoon.

"Please state your full name!" stated Mr. Gronert.

"My name is Joseph Salandra!"

"Do you reside in the County?"

"Yes I do!"

"Do you know the man that is on trial, Albert Williams?" asked Mr. Gronert.

"I only know him as Feets."

"Where and when did you first meet him?"

Joe became tense, and answered in a slightly higher pitched voice.

"I met him several weeks ago for the first time at Squints Place on Mason Street."

"Is he in this courtroom?"

"Yes," answered Joe, feeling slightly uncomfortable.

A bead of perspiration showed on his brow.

"Can you point him out?"

"Yes," said Joe as he pointed to Feets.

"That's him over there."

"Let the record show that the witness has pointed to the defendant."

"Relax. Take a drink of water!" whispered the Prosecuting Attorney attempting to set Joe at ease.

"Is there anything else that you can tell us about

him?"

"Yes! When I met Feets, I knew that I had seen him before. I first saw him at the Jungle Inn Club located over the state line in Pennsylvania. I was not introduced to him at that time, but some friends that had gone with me to have some fun, pointed him out and said that he was the Manager."

"What was Squint Fredrics relationship with Mr. Williams?"

"He acted like he was Squints boss. But Squint never told me that "Feets" was his boss."

"Thank you for your testimony Mr. Salandra."

"I'm through with this witness!"

The defense attorney passed on questioning Joe.

"You are excused," said Judge Griffen.

"Call your next witness," stated Judge Griffen.

"The prosecution calls Mr. Sal Mariner."

Sal is one of the two who confronted the barber after Squints body was found and told him that the Detroit mob had a hand in the killing.

Sal was sworn in.

"Mr. Mariner, do you know the defendant Mr. Williams?" asked Mr. Gronert.

"Yes!"

"Where do you know him from?"

"He is a neighbor of mine in Detroit!"

"How did you come to be arrested here in Trumbull County?"

"I came here to visit a sick friend!"

"Who is this sick friend?" asked Mr. Gronert.

"I would rather not say!"

"Isn't it true that you came here at the request of the mob in Detroit, to send a message to the city by blowing up Squint Fredrics establishment?"

"No! You already have the man in jail that did that!"

"That is true," said Mr. Gronert, "but didn't you hire him and give him the dynamite to do the job?"

"I never hired or gave any dynamite to anyone!"

Mister Gronert walked back to his desk, picked up a form and returned to the witness.

"I have a statement here from one Mugsy Milaus who is willing to testify that you hired him and that you gave him the materials he would need and that you paid him twenty-five thousand dollars to blow up the establishment. Furthermore, the police department searched your car and found residue from the dynamite that you hauled in the trunk of your car."

"Do you deny any of this?"

"I need to talk to my lawyer!"

"That is a good idea," stated Mr. Gronert.

"I'm through with this witness!"

"Do you wish to cross examine the witness Mr. Mastol?" asked Judge Griffen.

"No your honor. He is not my client!"

"Bailiff, place Mr. Mariner in custody!" stated Judge

Griffen.

The trial was an open and shut case. All the evidence pointed to the defendant.

The defense did not have much to say being that the evidence against Albert Williams was solid. Mr. Gronert did not leave any openings in his presentation to allow the defense to step in.

The defense began to work the jury on Tuesday to obtain any leniency that they could garner in the sentence. After Mr. Gronert presented his summation, the trial was sealed. The defenses efforts were hopeless and did nothing to change the minds of the Court.

The headlines in the Wednesday evening edition of our local newspaper announced the conviction of Albert Williams and that sentencing would be announced in one week. The following week the court announced that Albert Williams had been sentenced and was being moved from the County Jail to the prison in Columbus. He was scheduled for execution in the electric chair at that facility.

The Mason Woods

Chapter 22

Fun Times

It was the fourth of July. Mom and Dad were excited about going to the Park to enjoy the neighbors who would be there and the fireworks at dusk.

Mom prepared a large picnic basket with chicken and potato salad for us. With all the windows opened the aroma of Moms fried chicken cooking filled the air outside the house. And Moms chicken was as good as it smelled.

At 9:00 AM we all piled into the old 1932 Ford and went to the Park on the West side of town. It was only a ten-minute drive. When we arrived, Mom instructed Johnny and I to find a picnic table in the shade not too far from where the car was parked. We scampered to find the ideal table. It was in the shade and not far from where the City Recreation Department was giving free lemonade and coffee to anyone in the Park. Close to the row of swings. We sat at the table waiting for Mom and Dad to arrive with the food.

"Boys, here! Take the pitcher and the coffee pot and go to the refreshment stand and tell Jimmy to fill them up. They have lemonade and coffee," said Mom.

The refreshment stand was a small tent. There were three huge coffee urns sitting on the front table. Behind and towards the back of the tent were five huge tanks of lemonade.

"Hi boys! I see you have a coffee pot and a pitcher. Let me fill those up for you!"

Jimmy filled them up and brought them to the front table.

"There you go! Enjoy the picnic!"

"Thank You," said Johnny.

When we returned Mom and Dad had placed a cover over the table and put the picnic basket on the table. Mom filled Dads cup with coffee and ours with ice-cold lemonade.

"Let's sit here and relax for a while. It is nice and cool in the shade with the breeze blowing," said Mom.

We sat in the shade enjoying the cool breeze and our ice cold drinks.

We discovered that there will be various competition with prizes sponsored by the Recreation Department.

This would begin at 1:00 PM. There were also two softball games and a hardball game on the three baseball diamonds across the street.

Near to our table were the grownup swings. These swings were suspended from a bar that was twenty feet above the ground. The chains that held the seats in place were extra heavy. There were eight swings in all.

"Let's go over to the swings Johnny."

"OK!"

After a half hour Mom called. We refilled the lemonade pitcher and the coffee pot again before we sat down to eat Moms delicious fried chicken and potato salad.

After telling Mom how good the meal was Johnny and I went to where the competition was going to be held. There was a large gathering of children from various parts of town. I did not recognize any of them. The children were split up into age groups and boys on one-side girls on the other. The various games began and went on for almost two hours. By that time the children were spent and had more activity then they wanted. The games ended and Johnny and I had not one prize. But we still enjoyed the camaraderie. We returned to the picnic table.

Mom and Dad were with several acquaintances that they had not seen for sometime and seemed to be having a good time exchanging stories. We said our hellos. Johnny and I recognized one of the gentlemen at the table. His name was Sam.

Sam having come to the USA from the same town in

Italy that Mom came from would occasionally stop by the house to spend a little time with Mom and Dad. Sam was one of those Italians that talked with his hands. More than most Italians. Most Italians that emphasized their speech using their hands would move their hands as they went along. Sam was unique. Sam's hands would begin moving long before the first word was uttered. After that first word it was Sam flailing with both arms in all directions head tilting from side to side as the words came out slowly.

Out of respect, Mom and Dad felt that it was our duty to sit in the room with our guest. As hard as we tried, we were never able to remain composed. Even if we tried to close our minds to what Sam was saying the arm movements made it impossible? Johnny and I would begin by just squirming, trying not to think about Sam with arms flailing as we sat there. We would begin with a controlled snicker. Eyes tearing like we were going to explode. Then it went into a controlled giggle. Always hoping that Sam would say something funny so that we could burst out uncontrollably releasing all the pent up emotion. If Johnny snickered and choked, I would snicker and choke a little louder. Still trying to gain control. Finally it was beyond control. We burst out laughing. Angrily Dad would tell us to leave the room and we could hear him apologize to Sam who would just brush it off as "They're just kids."

After Sam left we would apologize to Mom and Dad for our behavior. But they understood. Dad said it was just Sam's way of expressing himself and there were times that he was at the verge of losing control also. But he never did. I believe Dad said that just to make us feel more at ease with the situation. On the other hand, I think he may have been playing a game too, insisting that we be there when Sam arrived. It was possible but far fetched that Dad wanted to see how long we could last. Timing us as it were.

Although we never talked about it, it became a game between Johnny and me. Each time that Sam came over, we would see who could last the longest before having to leave the room. It was usually a draw. We couldn't leave fast enough.

Before being asked to sit at the picnic table, we said hello to Sam and that we were going to go over to watch the ball games and would be back in an hour. We walked over to the baseball diamonds. We spent fifteen minutes at each diamond. None of the games drew our interest. We decided to go back to the picnic table and go on the nearby swings.

Mom and Dads visitors were gone. Mom was making sandwiches with the left over chicken so that we would have some food to keep us satisfied till the fireworks.

Dad whistled for us to come to the picnic table.

Johnny and I then went to get a pitcher of lemonade and pot of coffee. When we returned the table was set and we had a chicken sandwich and leftover potato salad.

The fireworks began at 9:00 PM sharp and lasted for approximately twenty minutes. The fireworks were spectacular. Especially the finale with the loud boom of the exploding rockets that seemingly came ever closer to the ground. At the conclusion we walked back to the car excited at how special the fireworks were. We got into the car and I fell asleep immediately and was awakened by Mom when we arrived home.

The following morning Johnny, Boo and I decided that we were not going to the Mason Woods. We opted to go down to the Creek and do some fishing.

In need of bait Johnny went into the garage and got a shovel and went to the damp soil behind the garage and began digging. Within five minutes we had a can with about twenty night crawlers. We gathered up our cane poles and got onto our bikes. We proceeded to the Creek that was on the out skirts of downtown near the waterfalls and Central Park.

It was tricky riding our bikes with the cane poles. Boo was having a problem with his cane pole.

"Boo! Let's stop and I'll take your pole and you can carry the worms."

"Alright!"

So I took his pole and gave him the bait can. We proceeded without trouble.

Our first stop was at the pond that lay before the river. The pond was filled with tadpoles and small frogs. There were also fish but mostly, they were small fish. The pond was used in the wintertime by ice skaters.

We slowly made our way around the pond, occasionally catching a tadpole or two and then releasing them back into the pond. The frogs were difficult to catch since our noisy approach would scare them into the water and away from the bank.

Finally we were at the edge of the river. Ready to try our luck at catching fish. After baiting our hooks we swung our lines out onto the water as far as they would go. It was now a waiting game.

Patience is required when fishing with cane poles. The idea is to watch the red and white float to detect any movement. If it moved, a fish was nosing around the bait. If the float sank, you had a fish on the line and the cane pole had to be raised skyward quickly in order to set the hook. After several minutes of waiting, Boos patience began to wear thin. He lifted his pole to check the bait and then placed it back in the river.

"Boo! You have to leave the bait in the water if you want to catch fish!" said Johnny.

"I know!"

After an hour of waiting with no fish biting our patience was gone.

"What do you guys say if we get out of here? It's too late in the day! The fish aren't around anymore," said Johnny.

"What do you think Boo?" I asked.

"Yah! I'm tired of this! Let's go do something else!"

We mounted our bikes and sluggishly peddled our way home. It was now two o'clock in the afternoon and a bit late to go out to the woods.

"I think that if to tired to do anything else today."

"Yah! I agree." said Johnny.

"See you guys tomorrow!" said Boo.

"OK!" responded Johnny.

The Mason Woods
Epilogue

All of the original immigrants that were introduced in the beginning of the book have passed on. Isabella (Our Dear Mother) passed in 1994. Vito(Our loving Father) passed in 1996. Anthony(Our close Uncle) followed Vito by one day.

Boo's son is the only contact with his family that I have had in these many years. His son Michael T. is a practicing physician.

Regarding the trial, Sal Mariner was found guilty and sentenced to ten years in the Ohio State Penitentiary. He was released in 1950. He returned to Detroit where he was found dead in an alley one year later the result of malnutrition. There was some controversy as to the nature of his death. Some say that the Purple Gang had gotten even. Officially, the Purple Gang was no longer in existence.

Mugsy Milaus the local who was accused of

bombing Squint Fredrics establishment pled for leniency as the result of turning witness for the prosecution in the case against Sal Mariner. He was found guilty of bombing Squint Fredrics establishment. His sentence was reduced by ten years for his help in the case against Sal Mariner. He received a sentence of 25 years. Mugsy died in the penitentiary in 1961. Mugsy was a frequent visitor to the barber shop. He lived across the street. His connections with various shady characters began when going to high school and working at the local newspaper distribution center.

Chief Ross was still on the Police Force as of 1985.

Mr. Ritchie the owner of the ice cream parlor never moved to Hawaii. His son died at Pearl Harbor during the Japanese attack of December 7, 1941. He sold his business and moved away with his wife to Florida.

Shortly after the end of WWII, Sid the theater Manager established a men's clothing facility on Main St. It was successful. He sold an excellent line of men's clothing at excellent prices. Sid retired from the business in 1979 due to health reasons and passed in 1981.

The East Side Barber Shop closed its doors in 1985 with the passing of Willie, the proprietor and sole operator for over 50 years.

Boo the close friend of Johnny and Phil died in an automobile accident coming from work in (1972??). A wife and two children survived him. Boo was 37 years old. 1935...1972.?

The small city where the events took place is NILES, OHIO.

Johnny lives in Henderson, Nevada. He is retired and living a comfortable life. Johnny is 76 years old. 1933.

Phil lives in Las Vegas, Nevada. He is retired and enjoying what Las Vegas has to offer. Phil is 78 years old. 1932.....